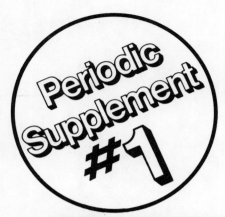

THE MINISTER'S LIBRARY

Cyril J. Barber

D1466019

BAKER BOOK HOUSE
Grand Rapids, Michigan

2.0764

Contents

Preface

The first printing of *The Minister's Library* met with a most cordial reception. For this I am profoundly thankful. Those who so kindly reviewed it in their denominational or professional journals invariably expressed a concern that "so important a reference tool be kept up to date." For this reason the publishers have requested me to prepare periodic supplements.

The importance of these supplements takes on added significance when we realize that in the period of time which has intervened since the completion of the first manuscript (June 1972), 117,000 new titles have been published in the United States alone. Of these new books 5,760 are in the area of religion.

With such a staggering volume of material coming from the presses of this and other lands, *selectivity* must continue to be the watchword of every busy pastor. This supplement, therefore, is designed to aid ministers and seminarians in their choice of the most important books. As in *The Minister's Library* the emphasis continues to be placed on expository tools and works which will enrich the pastor's personal life and ministry.

These supplements will continue to meet the need of the busy minister who, when he visits his local Christian book store, fails to find what he is looking for. By being aware of what has been published he can then request that certain books be ordered for him. In this respect these updatings will save a pastor time, help him evaluate the books that are available, and "serve as an invaluable aid when new purchases are to be made and other volumes added. They will soon repay the purchaser many times over in time saved and through avoidance of bad selections."[1]

In scanning the output of the past three years it will be observed that relatively few expository works have been written. And of these fewer still are from an evangelical perspective. On the other hand, there has been a veritable deluge of books on the occult, oriental mysticism, and other pagan religions. Inasmuch as *The Minister's Library* is geared to the needs of the Bible teacher and preacher, only a few of the representative titles in these other areas have been included.

Once again I am indebted to my friends and colleagues who have encouraged and helped me in the preparation of this supplement. To them I express my very real thanks.

Cyril J. Barber
Rosemead, California
June 1975

[1] Dr. Merrill F. Unger, Foreword to *The Minister's Library* (1974).

Chapter 1

BIBLE COMMENTARIES AND GENERAL REFERENCE WORKS

The Biblical Expositor. Edited by C. F. H. Henry. Philadelphia: A. J. Holman Co., 1973.

Formerly issued in three volumes in 1960; now available in an unabridged format in one volume. Designed to help laymen acquire a grasp of the "living theme of the great Book." Replete with essays relating to important Biblical themes. 220.7.B47 1973

Eerdmans' Handbook to the Bible. Edited by David Alexander and Patricia Alexander. Grand Rapids: Wm. B. Eerdmans Publishing Co., 1973.

†Edited in conjunction with a team of British scholars. Devoted to making the Bible more meaningful to readers. Part I consists of a general introduction to people and places mentioned in Bible times. Part II follows the OT narrative; Part III the NT; and Part IV is an index to a wide variety of themes. The chronology it follows will not be acceptable to all, and at times adheres to principles of interpretation long identified with liberal higher criticism. Lavishly illustrated. 220.02'02.ER1 1973

The Living Bible Concordance. Poolesville, MD: Poolesville Presbyterian Church, 1973.

A complete concordance to Kenneth Taylor's paraphrase of the Bible. 220.2.L75

Theological Dictionary of the Old Testament. Edited by G. Johannes Botterweck and Helmer Ringgren. Translated by John T. Willis. In process. Grand Rapids: Wm. B. Eerdmans Publishing Co., 1974–.

†This work is destined to become in the OT what *TDNT* is in the NT. Concentrates on key Hebrew and Aramaic words and seeks to determine their meaning in the culture of the times before developing their theological significance. The words are given in transliterated form, making this set easy to use—even by those with little knowledge of Hebrew. Scheduled for twelve vols. Extremely valuable. 221.3.T34

Unger, Merrill Frederick. *Unger's Guide to the Bible*. Wheaton: Tyndale House Publishers, 1974.

Contains a book-by-book survey of the Bible, a Bible dictionary, and a concordance. Of real value to laymen. 220.07.UN3G

Beegle, Dewey M. *Scripture, Tradition, and Infallibility*. Grand Rapids: Wm. B. Eerdmans Publishing Co., 1973.

†This new edition of *The Inspiration of Scripture* carries a Foreword by F.F. Bruce. Covers recent trends in Roman Catholic thought, and updates the author's attack on Fundamentalists and evangelicals who believe in an inerrant Bible. His emphasis centers in distinguishing between primary and secondary revelation and involves a denial of the authority of the Scriptures. 220.13.B395 1973

Miller, Donald G. *The Authority of the Bible*. Grand Rapids: Wm. B. Eerdmans Publishing Co., 1972.

Two sections are especially worthy of serious attention: "The Authority of the Bible over Christian Experience," and "The Biblical Basis of the Authority of the Church." 220.13.M61

*Montgomery, John Warwick, ed. *God's Inerrant Word*. Minneapolis: Bethany Fellowship, 1974.

Chapters by leading evangelical scholars on both sides of the Atlantic. Tackles and counters the claim of Beegle in *Scripture, Tradition, and Infallibility* that the Bible contains errors.
220.13.M76

Newport, John P., and **William Cannon.** *Why Christians Fight over the Bible.* Nashville: T. Nelson, 1974.

A dispassionate treatment of the differences between the various forms of theological "liberalism" and conservative beliefs. Includes a treatment of the rift already appearing between conservatives and the New Evangelicals. Most helpful. 220.6'6.N42

Olsson, Karl A. *Find Yourself in the Bible.* Minneapolis: Augsburg Publishing House, 1974.

Growing out of the author's own experience, this monograph highlights the place for and importance of group Bible study in the life of the church. 220.07.OL8

***Skilton, John H.,** ed. *Studying the New Testament Today.* The New Testament Student. Nutley, NJ: Presbyterian and Reformed Publishing Co.. 1974.

Contains excellent chapters on the inspiration and authority of the NT Scriptures, the place of the Greek text in preaching, and some indispensable books in NT research. De-

serves careful reading by all expositors. 225.07.S3

Wycliffe Bible Encyclopedia. Edited by Charles F. Pfeiffer, Howard F. Vos, and John Rea. 2 vols. Chicago: Moody Press, 1975.

The combined efforts of two hundred evangelical scholars make this handy reference volume an indispensable asset to both pastors and laymen. Included in it is the latest archaeological, historical, and philological research. The articles are brief and accurate. 220.3.W97

**The Zondervan Pictorial Encyclopedia of* *the Bible.* Edited by Merrill C. Tenney, *et al.* 5 vols. Grand Rapids: Zondervan Publishing House, 1975.

The product of more than ten years of research and preparation, this work contains articles by more than 240 evangelical scholars—many of international repute—covering a wide variety of Biblical and extra-Biblical subjects. A careful perusal of these well-illustrated volumes leaves little doubt that this encyclopedia is destined to become a major work for evangelicals for many years to come. 220.3.Z7

Creation, Science, and Religion

Coppedge, James F. *Evolution: Possible or Impossible?* Grand Rapids: Zondervan Publishing House, 1973.

A new approach to an old problem. Utilizes recent discoveries involving proteins and DNA, and provides evidence which militates against the traditional evolutionary theory. 575.01'62.C79

***Custance, Arthur C.** *Without Form and Void.* The Doorway Papers. Grand Rapids: Zondervan Publishing House, 1974.

The first of a ten-volume series designed to integrate the author's vast anthropological studies with the Biblical record. 215.C96

Patten, Donald W., Ronald R. Hatch, and **Loren C. Steinhaver.** *The Long Day of Joshua*

and Six Other Catastrophes. Seattle: Pacific Meridian Publishing Co., 1973.

Another valuable work on Christian evidence showing the close kinship between science and the Scriptures, and between ancient history and religion and the Biblical narrative of the OT. 904.5.P27

Rehwinkel, Alfred Martin. *The Wonder of Creation: An Exploration of the Origin and Splendors of the Universe.* Minneapolis: Bethany Fellowship, 1974.

Readers of *The Flood* will welcome the Biblical and scientific evidence which the author marshals to support his belief in special creation. 213.R26

Bible Versions
(Incl. History of Translations)

The Holy Bible. *The New International Version: The New Testament.* Grand Rapids: Zondervan Publishing House, 1973.

From a widely representative group of evangelical scholars comes this easy-to-read,

contemporary translation. 225.52.N42 1973

The New Oxford Annotated Bible. Edited by Herbert May and Bruce M. Metzger. New York: Oxford University Press, 1974.

†This revision of a decade-old "study Bible" contains few additional notes. The major change is the new, second edition of the NT. The notes reflect the critical bias of the editors. 220.52'04.OX2.R32 1974

Coggan, Donald. *Word and World.* London: Hodder and Stoughton, 1971.

In fine literary style the former Archbishop of York (now of Canterbury) discourses on the place of the Bible in determining the principles by which one may govern his life. An important contribution to one's understanding of the doctrine of Biblical relevancy. 220.5'09.C65

Frei, Hans W. *The Eclipse of Biblical Narrative.* New Haven: Yale University Press, 1974.

After tracing the change which took place in Biblical hermeneutics in the eighteenth and nineteenth centuries, Frei shows how this resulted in a loss of realism in the reading of the text. Insightful. 220.63'09.F87

Interpretation and Criticism of the Bible

Berkouwer, Gerrit Cornelis. *Holy Scripture.* Studies in Dogmatics. Grand Rapids: Wm. B. Eerdmans Publishing Co., 1975.

This work will most assuredly be read by theologians of all persuasions. It will also take its place among the most complete defenses of the authority of the Scriptures and become a leading text in this area for many years to come. 220.6.B45

Geisler, Norman L., and **William E. Nix.** *From God to Us.* Chicago: Moody Press, 1974.

Based on the well-known and widely used *General Introduction to the Bible,* this popularization of the material is ideal for use in adult Bible study groups. 220.6.G36F 1974

Morris, Henry Madison. *The Bible Has the Answer.* Grand Rapids: Baker Book House, 1973.

Basing his approach on a question-and-answer method, the author covers a wide variety of themes ranging from "The Word of God" to "Things to Come," and includes sections on "Misunderstood Bible Characters" and "Christian Holidays." 220.6'6.M83

Pink, Arthur Walkington. *The Doctrine of Revelation.* Grand Rapids: Baker Book House, 1975.

Based on articles from *Studies in Scripture,* these chapters draw attention to God's revelation of Himself in creation, the moral nature of man, history, the incarnation, and the Scriptures. The material probes many of modern man's dilemmas and shows that only in the revelation of God can man understand His all-wise providence. 220.6.P65

Old Testament

Archer, Gleason. *Old Testament Introduction.* Revised ed. Chicago: Moody Press, 1974.

A definitive study which in this revision perpetuates the finest conservative scholarship. A *must* for evangelicals who wish to have an intelligent grasp of the OT. 221.61.AR2 1974

Brockington, L. H. *The Hebrew Text of the Old Testament.* Malta: St. Paul's Press, 1973.

A discussion of the text used to support the NEB translation of the OT. One important feature of this work is the record of all variants (whether in pointing, word division, or text) from the third edition of Kittel's *Biblia Hebraica.* 221.4.B78

Noth, Martin. *A History of Pentateuchal Traditions.* Translated by Bernhard W. Andersen. Englewood Cliffs: Prentice-Hall, 1972.

Published posthumously, this source-critical work shows no awareness of trends in OT study over the past decade. 221.1'066.N81

Orlinsky, Harry Mayer. *Essays in Biblical Culture and Bible Translation.* New York: Ktav Publishing House, 1974.

This book, by a renowned Hebraist, contains a wide variety of essays which have been collected and published by his students. 220.6.OR5

Rad, Gerhard von. *Wisdom in Israel.* Nashville: Abingdon Press, 1972.

†Investigates the wisdom literature of ancient Judaism and attempts to correlate the place of knowledge in the religious experience of God's people. 222.1'066.R11

Walters, Peter. *The Text of the Septuagint: Its Corruptions and Their Emendations.*

Edited by D. W. Gooding. Cambridge: At the University Press, 1973.

An excellent prolegomena to the critical text of the LXX. Brings up to date Thackery's *Grammar of the Old Testament in Greek.* 221.48.W17

New Testament

Barclay, William. *Many Witnesses, One Lord.* Grand Rapids: Baker Book House, 1973.

While designed to show the diversity of viewpoints existing in the NT, the writer exhibits something of his own ambivalence to crucial areas of theology by alternately defending and then detracting from the Person of Christ. 225.6.B23

Current Issues in Biblical and Patristic Interpretation. Studies in Honor of Merrill C. Tenney. Edited by Gerald F. Hawthorne. Grand Rapids: Wm. B. Eerdmans Publishing Co., 1975.

A *Festschrift* honoring one whose lifetime of dedication to NT scholarship has resulted in a harvest of achievements. Covers a wide range of subjects—historical, Biblical and patristic, and theological. 225.6'6.T25.H31

Martin, Ralph Philip. *New Testament Foundations: A Guide for Christian Students.* Grand Rapids: Wm. B. Eerdmans Publishing Co., 1975.

†Scheduled for 2 volumes, volume 1 is devoted to a consideration of the Gospel records. The material is designed for students and is fully abreast of the latest trends in critical scholarship. Martin's handling of the teaching of the Gospels per se is the weakest part of the book. The background material (pp. 53-116), however, is handled with consummate skill. 225.6'6.M36

Davies, William David. *The Gospel and the Land.* Berkeley: University of California Press, 1974.

An important study dealing with the significance of the land of Palestine in Judaism, past and present. 225.8.D28. (Alt. DDC 236)

The Evangelical Theological Society. *New Directions in New Testament Study.* Edited by Richard N. Longenecker and Merrill C. Tenney. Grand Rapids: Zondervan Publishing House, 1974.

Contains papers of exceptional quality presented at the 1973 meeting of the E.T.S. 225.EV1 1974

Finegan, Jack. *Encountering New Testa-*

ment Manuscripts. Grand Rapids: Wm. B. Eerdmans Publishing Co., 1974.

A well-written, exciting excursus into the realm of NT textual criticism. Combines the fascinating saga of manuscript discoveries with the techniques of translation. 225.61.F49

*Gromacki, Robert Glenn. *New Testament Survey.* Grand Rapids: Baker Book House, 1974.

Of primary value as a collegiate text, this book nevertheless deserves a place in the pastor's library. Portrays not only *what* happened in NT times, but also explains *why,* and describes the way in which it became a part of the inspired writer's record. 225.6.G89

Hunter, Archibald Macbride. *Probing the New Testament.* Richmond: John Knox Press, 1972.

Published in the United Kingdom under the title *Exploring the New Testament* (1971), this work concentrates attention on words, phrases, or meanings in the NT, and discusses their relevance to people today. 225.61.H91

Kümmel, Werner George. *The New Testament: The History of the Investigation of Its Problems.* Translated by S. McLean Gilmour and Howard C. Kee. Nashville: Abingdon Press, 1972.

This historic survey into the problems of NT study—from ancient times to 1930—is of value for its general discussion and the lengthy quotations from leading scholars. It is not evaluative and manifests a tendency to accept the theories of others without adequate investigation. 225.6.K96

———.*Introduction to the New Testament.* Translated by Howard Clark Kee. Nashville: Abingdon Press, 1975.

†A complete revision of the former edition with emphasis on new trends in NT research, an examination of the literary character and theological purpose of the NT documents, and updated surveys on the origin of the canon, the history of the text, and the present state of NT criticism. 225.61.K96

La Sor, William Sanford. *The Dead Sea Scrolls and the New Testament.* Grand Rapids: Wm.B. Eerdmans Publishing Co., 1973.

Marshals a vast amount of material and presents it with fairness and skill. Of particular interest is the comparison between the early church and the Qumran community. 225.4.L33

Mueller, Walter. *Grammatical Aids for Students of New Testament Greek.* Grand Rapids: Wm. B. Eerdmans Publishing Co., 1972.

Designed to supplement a regular grammar. Its chief value is for those who either have no prior knowledge of the language or stand in need of a "refresher" course. 487.4. M88

Vos, Howard Frederick. *Beginnings in the New Testament.* Chicago: Moody Press, 1973.

A useful work for laymen or Bible discussion groups. 225.6. V92

Wenham, John William. *Christ and the Bible.* Downers Grove, IL: InterVarsity Press, 1972.

The first of four volumes on the nature, interpretation, and application of Scripture, this one is designed to update and supplement the work of B. B. Warfield. Attempts to show that belief in the Bible comes from faith in Christ, not *vice versa.* 220.6. W48

Special Subjects in the Bible

Bruce, Frederick Fyvie. *Answers to Questions.* Grand Rapids: Zondervan Publishing House, 1973.

Contains candid replies to frequently asked questions. Insightful. 220.8. B83

*Culver, Robert Duncan. *Toward a Biblical View of Civil Government.* Chicago: Moody Press, 1974.

A "landmark" work which deserves a place in every church library. 220.832. C89

Epstein, Louis M. *The Jewish Marriage Contract: A Study in the Status of the Woman in Jewish Law.* New York: Arno Press, 1973.

First published in 1927, this volume contributes immensely to our knowledge of marriage in OT times. 346.01. EP8 1973

Ferguson, Walter W. *Living Animals of the Bible.* New York: Charles Scribner's Sons, 1974.

A magnificently illustrated volume containing paintings of animals (including mammals, birds, etc.) mentioned in the Bible and still living today. The Hebrew names are given with the English equivalent followed by their Latin *phila,* and selected passages of Scripture in which they are mentioned. 220.859. F38

Oates, Wayne Edward. *The Psychology of Religion.* Waco, TX: Word Books, 1973.

Realizing that the disciplines of theology and psychology have long been at enmity with one another, Oates attempts to define a common approach to human life and provide a common meeting ground for both. He is correct in assuming that psychology can serve as the "handmaid" of the theologian, but manifests a distinct weakness in his understanding of the nature of man. Discusses such issues as mysticism, LSD, operant conditioning, the counter culture, and demon possession. 200'.1. OA8

Oden, Thomas C. *Game Free.* New York: Harper and Row, 1974.

†An attempt to apply the Scriptures in terms of Transactional Analysis terms. Oden makes important observations and correctives but fails to emphasize the need for any redemptive act. 158.2. OD2

*Ryken, Leland. *The Literature of the Bible.* Grand Rapids: Zondervan Publishing House, 1974.

Deals admirably with all the categories of modern literary criticism, and thus adds new meaning to the study of the Bible. 220.88. R98 (Alt. DDC 809.93522)

*Ryrie, Charles Caldwell. *You Mean the Bible Teaches That. . . .* Chicago: Moody Press, 1974.

Clear, concise chapters on subjects such as civil obedience, women's lib, divorce, situation ethics, abortion, etc. Of real value to those who are disturbed over today's ethical dilemmas. 220.817. R99

*Unger, Merrill Frederick. *Biblical Demonology: A Study of the Spiritual Forces Behind the Present World Unrest.* Wheaton: Scripture Press, 1974.

First published in 1952. Exposes the fallacies inherent in Satanism and explains the resurgence of interest in the occult. 220.813. UN3

Old Testament

Cohen, H. Hirsch. *The Drunkenness of Noah.* University, AL: University of Alabama Press, 1974.

†A scholarly study by a rabbi whose extensive research into the social conditions prevailing at the time of the deluge makes a distinct contribution to our knowledge of this era of history. Includes a chapter on man as

God's representative and the sin and affliction of Cain. 221.8.C66

Hassel, Gerhard F. *Old Testament Theology: Basic Issues in the Current Debate.* Grand Rapids: Wm. B. Eerdmans Publishing Co., 1972.

A critical appraisal of the history and methodology of contemporary OT study. Hassel rejects the *religionsgeschichttiche Schule,* and the *Weltanschauung* of modern rationalism. Also repudiates the "confession" approach of some European writers, and corrects many ideas inherent in *Heilsgeshichte.* Exposes the inadequacies of these theories to OT theology and then lays a foundation for a constructive approach to the teaching of the OT. 221.823.H27

Kaiser, Walter C., Jr. *The Old Testament and Contemporary Preaching.* Grand Rapids: Baker Book House, 1973.

A popular presentation of the relevance of the OT in developing a meaningful philosophy of life. 221.6'6.K12

*The Law and the Prophets: Old Testament Studies Prepared in Honor of Oswald Thompson Allis. Edited by John H. Skilton. Philadelphia: Presbyterian and Reformed Publishing Co., 1974.

These essays, in honor of one of the great OT scholars of all time, cover a wide variety of themes by leading evangelical scholars. 221.8.AL5.L41

McKenzie, John L. *A Theology of the Old Testament.* Garden City, NY: Doubleday and Co., 1974.

†This scholarly work by a Roman Catholic theologian approaches the OT on the basis of its cultus, revelation, history, nature, wisdom, institutions, and eschatology. The author sees no vital connection between OT theology and the development of NT doctrine. 221.082.M19

New Testament

Barrett, Charles Kingsley. *New Testament Essays.* London: SPCK, 1972.

Studies giving evidence of deep scholarship and awareness of the contemporary NT debate. 227.8.B27

_____. *The Signs of an Apostle.* Philadelphia: Fortress Press, 1972.

An in-depth treatment of what was involved in apostleship in the first century A.D. 262.72.B27

Berry, Harold J. *Gems from the Original.*

Lincoln, NE: Back to the Bible Broadcast, 1972.

Brief, devotional studies on such topics as "The Believer's Old Nature," "The Great Commission." Helpful to laymen; or of value for ideas when called upon to give an occasional talk. 255.84.B45

Gunther, John Jacob. *Paul: Messenger and Exile:* Valley Forge: Judson Press, 1972.

A study in the chonology of Paul's life and letters. 227.094.G95

_____. *St. Paul's Opponents and Their Background.* Leiden, The Netherlands: E. J. Brill, 1974.

This seminal study finds Paul's opponents closer to Essenism than to any other school or sect (including Pharisaism) in Judaism. 227.08.G95

Ladd, George Eldon. *A Theology of the New Testament.* Grand Rapids: Wm. B. Eerdmans Publishing Co., 1974.

An important contribution covering the Synoptics, Johannine, and Pauline writings, and including material from the Acts and catholic epistles. 225.823.L12

Long, A. A. *Hellenistic Philosophy: Stoics, Epicureans, Sceptics.* New York: Charles Scribner's Sons, 1974.

Provides a vivid portrayal of the intellectual climate in Greek cities visited by the apostle Paul, and forms a valuable backdrop to the study of many of his letters. 180.L25

Lehman, Chester K. *Biblical Theology: New Testament.* Scottsdale, PA: Herald Press, 1974.

Not since G. Vos's treatment has anything quite like this been attempted. Lehman's approach differs from G. E. Ladd's *Theology of the New Testament.* This is not an in-depth study and will probably be most widely used in Bible colleges. 225.823.L52

Perrin, Norman. *A Modern Pilgrimage in New Testament Christology.* Philadelphia: Fortress Press, 1974.

†These essays apply the author's "process theology" to the Synoptic Gospels in the vain hope of drawing from them a NT Christology. 225.8.P41

Schmithals, Walter. *Paul and the Gnostics.* Translated by John E. Steely. Nashville: Abingdon Press, 1972.

†Continuing the author's study begun in *Gnosticism in Corinth,* this work applies his earlier material to the conditions of the church and the development of Pauline theology. 227.S6

Shires, Henry M. *Finding the Old Testament in the New*. Philadelphia: Westminster Press, 1974.

†Builds upon previous works and enhances our knowledge of the way the NT uses the OT. Written in a style that is easily comprehended. Its approach to and handling of problem areas is forthright and helpful. 225.84.SH6

Stanley, David Michael. *Boasting in the Lord*. New York: Paulist Press, 1974.

A theological examination of Paul's prayers which probes the heart of Paul's life and reveals not only his personal commitment to the Lord, but the secret of his success as well. 227.08.S2

Wiles, Gordon P. *Paul's Intercessory Prayers: The Significance of the Intercessory Prayer Passages in the Letters of St. Paul.*

New York: Cambridge University Press, 1974.

A scholarly work limited to an investigation of the supplications by which Paul presented the needs of others to the Lord. While complicated by the intrusion of "liturgical" material, this book may nevertheless be studied with profit. 227.08.P89.W64

Ziesler, J. A. *The Meaning of Righteousness in Paul: A Linguistic and Theological Enquiry*. New York: Cambridge University Press, 1972.

A study reflecting the writer's desire to come to grips with this facet of Pauline theology. His goal is to overcome categorical difficulties underlying much of the present debate. He shows that *dikatoō* is used relatively, often with the meaning "to acquit," and that *dikaios* frequently has a behavioral meaning. 234.7.Z6

Bible Geography, Archaeology, and Customs

*Avi-Yonah, Michael. *The Holy Land*. New York: Holt, Rinehart and Winston, 1972.

Designed for use by visitors to Palestine, also of interest and value to those who are not able to tour the Holy Land. Its pictures —black-and-white as well as color—are extremely beautiful and portray in detail the customs and culture of the people in the cities, as well as in the out-of-the-way places seldom visited by tourists. 913.3.AV5

*Baly, Denis A. *The Geography of the Bible*. New and rev. ed. New York: Harper and Row, 1974.

A revision of an outstanding work on Biblical geography. Includes not only matters of physical geography, but geological formations, climatology, topography, and flora and fauna as well. 220.91.B34 1974.

Couasnon, Charles. *The Church of the Holy Sepulchre in Jerusalem*. New York: Oxford University Press. 1974.

A beautifully illustrated, detailed history. 726.5.C83

Jones, Clifford M. *New Testament Illustrations*. The Cambridge Bible Commentary. Cambridge: At the University Press, 1966.

A useful, pictographic record designed to add a new dimension to NT study. 225.91.J71

*Kenyon, Kathleen Mary, *Digging Up Jerusalem*. New York: Praeger Publishers, 1974.

An important work on the history of the Holy City by a renowned archaeologist who, during 1961-67, excavated portions of Jerusalem. 913.33.J47.K42

Lawlor, John Irving. *The Nabataeans in Historical Perspective*. Grand Rapids: Baker Book House, 1974.

A unique volume making available a vast amount of material on these NT inhabitants of OT Edom. 220.93.N11.L42

May, Herbert Gordon, ed. *Oxford Bible Atlas*. 2d ed. New York: Oxford University Press, 1974.

†Lavishly illustrated with color maps and plates, this thorough revision of the 1962 edition contains data showing the vegatation and rainfall in Bible lands and information pertaining to the most recent archaeological findings. The material reflects the "left-wing" position of the contributors. 220.9.OX2.M45 1974

*Reader's Digest Association. *Great People of the Bible and How They Lived*. Pleasantville, NY: Reader's Digest Association, 1974.

A beautifully illustrated, comprehensive, and generally reliable portrayal of the customs and culture of Palestine from Abraham to the apostle Paul. 220.91.R22

*Vaux, Roland de. *Archaeology and the Dead Sea Scolls*. London: The British Academy, 1973.

A detailed discussion of the site of ancient Qumran, the authenticity of the Dead Sea material, and the relevance of these studies to Biblical scholarship. Roman Catholic. 221.44.V46

Vos, Howard Frederick. *Beginnings in Bible Geography.* Chicago: Moody Press, 1973.
A popular presentation which admirably lends itself to use by discussion groups. 220.91.V92

*****Wiseman, Donald J., ed.** *Peoples of the Old Testament.* Oxford: Clarendon Press, 1973.

A brilliant series of essays dealing with those nations in the ancient Near East whose borders or activities impinged upon God's chosen people. Each chapter contains a full discussion of the history, religion, customs, and literature of the race under consideration. 2w1.91.W75

Yamauchi, Edwin M. *The Stones and the Scriptures.* Philadelphia: J. B. Lippincott Co., 1972.
A summary of archaeological evidence and its relationship to OT and NT studies. Up to date and informative. 221.93.Y1

Bible Characters

*****Barber, Cyril John.** *God Has the Answer . . . to Your Problems.* Grand Rapids: Baker Book House, 1974.
Definitive (though abridged) studies on thirteen men of the Bible who confronted problems common to everyone at one time or another. Explores their resources and shows *how* and *why* they overcame their difficulties. 220.92.B23

Barclay, William. *Ambassador for Christ: The Life and Teaching of the Apostle Paul.* Valley Forge: Judson Press, 1974.
First published in 1951, this book surveys the travels and ministry of the apostle Paul. 227.092.P28.B23

Beegle, Dewey M. *Moses, the Servant of Yahweh.* Grand Rapids: Wm. B. Eerdmans Publishing Co., 1972.
†Combines a study of Moses' personality with a running commentary on Exodus and occasional excursions into parallel material in the Pentateuch. Of importance for the insights it contains, but manifests a strong reliance upon the works of W. F. Albright. The main strength of Beegle's work is his ability to relate the customs and culture of the ancient Near East to his "biography" of Moses. 221.92.M85.B39

Brownrigg, Ronald. *The Twelve Apostles.* New York: Macmillan Co., 1974.
A well-written but shallow portrayal of the lives and legends of the apostles combining the Biblical records with historical interpretations and artist's impressions. 225.92.B82

Deen, Edith. *All the Bible's Men of Hope.* Garden City, NY: Doubleday and Co., 1974.
A popularly written work which appropriately draws attention to the hope which motivated those whose lives are forever enshrined in Holy Writ. Shows that this belief (or "hope") was not an abstraction, but a powerful internal dynamic. 220.92.D36

*****Hiebert, David Edmond.** *Personalities Around Paul.* Chicago: Moody Press, 1973.
A superb treatment of the men and women who labored with the apostle Paul. Helpful to any preacher desiring to expound the Acts or the Pauline Epistles. 227.092.H53

Tatford, Frederick A. *Prophet from the Euphrates—Balaam and His Parables.* Eastbourne, Sussex, Eng.: Prophetic Witness Publishing House, 1973.
A perceptive work which combines an exposition of Balaam's oracles with an application to the needs of people today. 221.92.B18.T18

Zeligs, Dorothy F. *Psychoanalysis and the Bible: a Study in Depth of Seven Leaders.* New York: Bloch Publishing Co., 1974.
†An important, though strongly Freudian, approach to the lives of Abraham, Jacob, Joseph, Samuel, Saul, David, and Solomon. 221.92.Z3

Bible History

*Anstey, Martin. *Chronology of the Old Testament*. Grand Rapids: Kregel Publications, 1973.

This prodigous work, first published in 1913 under the title, *The Romance of Bible Chronology* remains of real value for the serious Bible student. 221.94.AN8

Larve, Gerald A. *Ancient Myth and Modern Man*. Englewood Cliffs: Prentice-Hall, 1975.

An examination of the way in which hero stories of the past are projected into the future and find their expression in personal attitudes and social values. 301.2.L32

Ringgren, Helmer. *Religions of the Ancient Near East*. Philadelphia: Westminster Press, 1973.

A well-researched survey of the religious beliefs of the Sumerian, Babylonian, Assyrian, and West-Semitic peoples. 299.9.R47

Schultz, Samuel J. *The Gospel of Moses*. New York: Harper and Row, 1974.

A refreshing survey stressing the grace of God in His dealings with Israel in OT times. 221.95.M85.SCH8

Yamauchi, Edwin M. *Pre-Christian Gnosticism: A Survey of Proposed Evidences*. Grand Rapids: Wm. B. Eerdmans Publishing Co., 1973.

A technical treatise revealing the extremely fluid state of gnostic study. 273.1.Y1

Chapter 2

OLD TESTAMENT

Historical Books

Davidson, Robert. *Genesis 1-11*. Cambridge Bible Commentary on the New English Bible. New York: Cambridge University Press, 1973.
†This "Prologue" to Genesis presents the material in the form of "myths" within a religious framework and seeks to see extra-Biblical tales behind the events of creation, the fall, the flood, and the tower of Babel. 221.11'07. D28 1-11

Jacob, Benno. *The First Book of the Bible: Genesis*. Translated and edited by Ernest I. Jacob and Walter Jacob. New York: Ktav Publishing House, 1974.
After rejecting the documentary hypothesis, the author breaks new ground as he correlates the rich heritage of Judaism with the text of Genesis. 222.11'07.J11 1974

***Livingstone, George Herbert.** *The Pentateuch in Its Cultural Environment*. Grand Rapids: Baker Book House, 1974.
This informative, well-illustrated book introduces the Bible student to the lives and times of the Patriarchs, analyzes the literature of the period, and provides a valuable critique of Near Eastern customs and culture. 222.1'09.L76

Mackintosh, Charles Henry. *Genesis to Deuteronomy: Notes on the Pentateuch*. Neptune, NJ: Loizeaux Brothers, 1974.
Now readers have in one volume the "Notes" of CHM which were originally published between 1880-82. 222.11'07.M21

***Whitcomb, John Clement, Jr.** *The World That Perished*. Grand Rapids: Baker Book House, 1973.
This supplement to *The Genesis Flood* and

companion volume of *The Early Earth* brings up to date the author's vast research into the primeval conditions prevailing on the earth before the deluge, as well as the changes which took place following the flood. 222.11'06.W58W 6-9

Schaeffer, Francis August. *Genesis in Space and Time: The Flow of Biblical History*. Downers Grove, IL: InterVarsity Press, 1972.
In grappling with the dilemmas facing modern man, Schaeffer correctly traces their origin to man's rejection of the early chapters of Genesis. The author from L'Abri explains their relevance in terms of the present day. 222.11.SCH1 1-11

Childs, Brevard S. *The Book of Exodus*. Philadelphia: Westminister Press, 1974.
Building upon the principles laid down in his *Biblical Theology in Crisis,* Childs applies them to the Book of Exodus and succeeds in providing his readers with a scholarly work which will be referred to for many years to come. 222.12'07.C43

***Cole, Robert Alan.** *Exodus: An Introduction and Commentary*. Tyndale Old Testament Commentaries. Downers Grove, IL: InterVarsity Press, 1973.
Basing his exposition primarily on the theology of Exodus, the writer succeeds in providing a brief, but valuable commentary on the text. 222.12'07.C67

Courville, Donovan A. *The Exodus Problem and Its Ramifications*. 2 vols. Loma Linda, CA: Challenge Books, 1971.
This critical examination of the chronological problems surrounding the Israelites and

their emancipation from Egypt gives evidence of careful inquiry and deserves careful reading on the part of those interested in the problems. 222.12'06.C83

Carmichael, Calum M. *The Laws of Deuteronomy.* Ithaca: Cornell University Press, 1974.
†A scholarly study showing that the Book of Deuteronomy is a carefully constructed, coherent treatise, written with a definite purpose in mind. 222.15'06.C21

Thompson, John Arthur. *Deuteronomy: An Introduction and Commentary.* Tyndale Old Testament Commentaries. Downers Grove, IL: InterVarsity Press, 1975.
A well-documented treatise, rich in Near Eastern culture, which ably expounds Moses' final messages to God's people. 222.15'07.T37

Gray, John. *Joshua, Judges and Ruth.* New Century Bible. Greenwood, SC: Attic Press, 1967.
†A highly critical treatment. 222.2'07.G79

Boling, Robert G. *The Anchor Bible: Judges.* Garden City, NY: Doubleday and Co., 1974.
†Manifesting a heavy dependence upon the LXX and the Qumran scrolls, Boling suc-

ceeds in providing his readers with enrichments from archaeological sources. Weak as an exposition, or as a work of exegesis. 222.3'07.B63

Mayes, A. D. H. *Israel in the Period of the Judges.* Studies in Biblical Theology, Second Series. London: SCM Press, 1974.
†This attack on Noth's amphictyonic concept views Israel's unity as purely theoretical. Mayes, however, concludes by admitting that the paucity of materials precludes the possibility of any final judgment. 222.3'06.M45

Ellul, Jacques. *The Politics of God and the Politics of Man.* Grand Rapids: Wm. B. Eerdmans Publishing Co., 1972.
Basing his political theory on the fact that the problems of our times are theological and not sociological, the writer shows from a study of II Kings how God has provided a "blueprint" for self-government in the Bible. Rewarding reading. 222.54'092.EL5

Ackroyd, Peter R. *I and II Chronicles, Ezra, Nehemiah.* Torch Bible Commentaries. London: SCM Press, 1973.
†Fully abreast of the latest scholarship, these brief studies survey the content of the post-exilic writings, and provide occasional helpful insights into problems in the text. 222.6'07.AC5

Poetic Writings

Rowley, Harold Henry. *Job.* New Century Bible. Greenwood, SC: Attic Press [1970].
†This scholarly study is of significance for its bibliographic notes rather than for its comments on the text. 223.1'07.R79

Anderson, A. A. *Psalms.* New Century Bible. 2 vols. Greenwood, SC: Attic Press [1972].
†A critical treatment, which does not capitalize on the research of Dahood and fails to meet the need of a good, modern exposition. 223.2'06.AN3

Anderson, Bernard W. *Out of the Depths: The Psalms Speak for Us Today.* Philadelphia: Westminster Press, 1974.
†Grounded in form-criticism and an existential theology. May nevertheless be read with profit by the discerning reader.

Kidner, Derek. *Psalms 1-72.* Tyndale Old Testament Commentaries. Downers Grove,

IL: InterVarsity Press, 1973.
This small volume condenses the fruit of scholarly inquiry of the past sixty years, and presents in layman's language an analysis of the different kinds of hymnic literature and the setting of the worship ritual of the ancient Israelites. 223.2'07.K53 1-72

McKane, William. *Proverbs, a New Approach.* Old Testament Library. Philadelphia: Westminster Press, 1970.
†An informative, but highly critical study. 223.7'07.M19

DeHaan, Richard, and **Herbert Vander Lugt.** *The Art of Staying Off Dead-end Streets.* Wheaton: Victor Books, 1974.
A practical study of Ecclesiastes. Ideal for laymen and Bible discussion groups. 223.8'07.D36

Gordis, Robert. *The Song of Songs and Lamentations: A Study, Modern Translation and Commentary.* Revised ed. New York:

Ktav Publishing House, 1974.

First published in 1954, these technical studies interpret these OT writings and provide numerous cultural and linguistic insights. Extensive documentation makes them ideal for the scholar, but minimizes their value for the busy pastor. 223.9'06.G65 1974

Kaiser, Otto. *Isaiah 13-39.* Old Testament Library. Translated by R. A. Wilson. Philadelphia: Westminster Press, 1974.

† An exacting study whose chief value lies in the relationship of Jewish expectation to her apocalyptic literature and the eventual removal of her hopes as a nation from the realm of history. 224.1'07.K12

Prophetic Books

*Lang, George Henry. *The Histories and Prophecies of Daniel.* Grand Rapids: Kregel Publications, 1974.

Based primarily on the RV, this premillennial, posttribulation work, by a leading Plymouth Brethren writer, combines extensive research with a comprehensive treatment of the prophetic Scriptures. 224.5'07.L25

Wolff, Hans Walter. *Hosea.* Philadelphia: Fortress Press, 1974.

† This form-critical study contains extensive footnotes and a wealth of grammatical insights. It will be of value to serious students of the OT. 224.7'07.W83

Tatford, Frederick A. *Prophet of Judgment Day.* Eastbourne, Sussex, Eng.: Prophetic Witness Publishing House, 1974.

A forthright presentation of the message of Joel with application to today and to what is still future. 224.8'07.T18

*Motyer, John Alexander. *The Day of the Lion. The Voice of the Old Testament.* Downers Grove, IL: InterVarsity Press, 1974.

A helpful examination of the Book of Amos which relates the message of this OT prophet to the needs of the present day. 224.9'07.M85

Tatford, Frederick A. *Prophet of Social Injustice.* Eastbourne, Sussex, Eng.: Prophetic Witness Publishing House, 1974.

In these pages Amos's judgment is expounded with clarity and insight. The timeliness of his message also receives skillful application. 224.9'07.T18

————. *Prophet of Edom's Doom.* Eastbourne, Sussex, Eng.: Prophetic Witness Publishing House, 1973.

A competent exposition of Obadiah's vision of Edom's demise. 224.91'07.T18

————. *Prophet of Messiah's Advent.* Eastbourne, Sussex, Eng.: Prophetic Witness Publishing House, 1974.

A discerning evaluation of the scope of Micah's prophecy. 224.93'07.T18

————. *Prophet of Royal Blood.* Eastbourne, Sussex, Eng.: Prophetic Witness Publishing House, 1973.

Long neglected, the message of Zephaniah is given careful treatment in this handy volume. 224.96'07.T18

Baldwin, Joyce. *Haggai, Zechariah, Malachi.* Tyndale Old Testament Commentaries. Downers Grove, IL: InterVarsity Press, 1972.

Brief, scholarly verse-by-verse comments with "Additional Notes" interspersed throughout the text. 224.97.B19

Tatford, Frederick A. *Prophet of the Restoration.* Eastbourne, Sussex, Eng.: Prophetic Witness Publishing House, 1972.

A summary of the Book of Haggai with sufficient pertinent data to stimulate lively discussions. 224.97'07.T18

*Morgan, George Campbell. *Malachi's Message for Today.* Grand Rapids: Baker Book House, 1972.

First published in 1898 under the title, *Wherein Have We Robbed God?* Applies the pertinent truths of Malachi's prophecy to the needs of our modern society. 224.99'07.M82

Tatford, Frederick A. *Prophet of the Reformation.* Eastbourne, Sussex, Eng.: Prophetic Witness Publishing House, 1972.

A concise exposition of Malachi's prophecy. Ideal for discussion groups. 224.99'07.T18

Chapter 3

NEW
TESTAMENT

Gospels and Acts

Goulder, Michael D. *Midrash and Lection in Matthew*. London: S.P.C.K., 1974.

†Following in the footsteps of Austin Farrer, the author dispenses with Q, and attempts to build a case for Matthew's Gospel being a Midrash of Mark. 226.2'06. G72

*Hendriksen, William. *Exposition of the Gospel According to Matthew*. New Testament Commentary. Grand Rapids: Baker Book House, 1973.

Following a comprehensive introduction the writer treats his readers to 900 pages of detailed exposition. His approach is geographic and his style pedantic. There is an elaborate explanation of the text and a full discussion of varying views. 226.2'07.H38

Hill, David. *The Gospel of Matthew*. New Century Bible. Greenwood, SC: Attic Press, 1972.

†A form-critical study which discusses recent developments in NT scholarship, followed by comments on the text of the RSV. The author does not expound the purpose of this Gospel and his treatment of Matthean theology beclouds the issues. 226.2'07.H55

Walvoord, John Flipse. *Matthew: Thy Kingdom Come*. Chicago: Moody Press, 1974.

In this book we have a modern, scholarly attempt to expound Matthew's Gospel *thematically*. While lacking a solid introduction this commentary deserves a place in the library of the expository Bible teacher and preacher. 226.2'07.W17

Farmer, William Reuben. *The Last Twelve Verses of Mark*. New York: Cambridge University Press, 1974.

An examination, first of the textual evidence for the ommission of the verses, and second, of the linguistic reasons for their inclusions. While the author advocates their retention, he leaves numerous questions unanswered. 226.3'06.F22 16:9-20.

*Hendriksen, William. *Exposition of the Gospel According to Mark*. New Testament Commentary. Grand Rapids: Baker Book House, 1975.

Making its own unique contribution to the study of Mark's Gospel, this work will be eagerly sought after by preachers of all persuasions. 226.3'07.H38

*Hiebert, David Edmond. *Mark: A Portrait of the Servant*. Chicago: Moody Press, 1974.

A reverent and insightful treatment which deserves the attention of the Bible teacher and expository preacher. 226.3'07.H53

*Lane, William L. *The Gospel According to Mark*. New International Commentary on the New Testament. Grand Rapids: Wm. B. Eerdmans Publishing Co., 1974.

Fully abreast of the latest research. Combines the exacting care of a philologist with the expertise of a theologian. 226.3'07.L24

Martin, Ralph Philip. *Mark: Evangelist and Theologian*. Grand Rapids: Zondervan Publishing House, 1973.

A scholarly assessment of the scope of Mark's Gospel with a suggestion for a new purpose and *Stiz im leben*. 226.3'06.M36

*Morris, Leon. *The Gospel According to St. Luke*. Tyndale New Testament Commentaries. Grand Rapids: Wm. B. Eerdmans Publishing Co., 1974.
A clear, forthright presentation of the facts surrounding the authorship and date of this Gospel, followed by almost 300 pages of exposition. A handy and helpful volume. 226.4'07.M83

*Barber, Cyril John. *Searching for Identity*. Chicago: Moody Press, 1975.
Thirteen studies based on men and women in John's Gospel. The writer integrates psychology with theology as he expounds the text. Designed for individual or group use. 226.5'092.B23

Kent, Homer Austin, Jr. *Light in the Darkness: Studies in the Gospel of John*. Grand Rapids: Baker Book House, 1974.
Of value for use with groups, this work adequately expounds the theme and content of John's Gospel. 226.5.K41

Lindars, Barnabas. *The Gospel of John*. New Century Bible. Greenwood, SC: Attic Press, 1973.
†This work is by far the most extensive and also the most radical to have been published in this series thus far. Lindars claims that the only valid interpretation of this Gospel is an existential one. He therefore searches for meaning behind the events recorded, but does so without treating the events as having actually taken place. 226.5'07.L64

*Rosscup, James E. *Abiding in Christ:*

Studies in John 15. Grand Rapids: Zondervan Publishing House, 1973.
An in-depth discussion of the apostle's teaching on abiding in Christ. Contains a full discussion of the problems and shows clearly the Christian's responsibility to live in love and obedience to the Lord. 226.5'07.R73 15:1-6

*Stedman, Ray C. *Secrets of the Spirit*. Old Tappan, NJ: Fleming H. Revell Co., 1975.
As an exposition of Christ's "Last Will and Testament," these studies (of John 14-17) ably treat the events which took place on the eve of the crucifixion. 226.5'07.S3 14-16

Kent, Homer Austin, Jr. *Jerusalem to Rome—Studies in Acts*. Grand Rapids: Baker Book House, 1972.
In recounting the beginning and expansion of the early church, the writer reveals the personal struggles of those who participated in the events recorded by Luke. The inclusion of discussion questions makes this an ideal volume for adult Bible study groups. 226.6'07.K41

Neil, William. *The Acts of the Apostles*. New Century Bible. Greenwood, SC: Attic Press, 1973.
While not written from an "evangelical" perspective, the writer manifests a conservative approach to the text and provides perceptive historical and theological sidelights on the events recorded by Luke. 225.6'07.N31

*Stedman, Ray C. *Birth of the Body*. Santa Ana, CA: Vision House Publishers, 1974.
A vibrant recounting of the early church's beginning and witness. The author shows how the power available to the early Christians is available today. The formula is found in Acts 1-12. 225.6'07.S3 1-12

Pauline Epistles

Black, Matthew. *Romans*. New Century Bible. Greenwood, SC: Attic Press, 1973.
†The comments, while perceptive, are too brief to be of great value. Of primary significance are the bibliographical notes scattered throughout the text. 227.1'07.B56

Johnson, Alan F. *The Freedom Letter*. Chicago: Moody Press, 1974.

A contemporary exposition of the theme and content of Paul's Roman epistle. 227.1'07.J63

*Lloyd-Jones, David Martyn. *Romans: An Exposition of Chapters 7:1—8:4. The Law: Its Functions and Limits*. Grand Rapids: Zondervan Publishing House, 1974.
This careful and detailed work is an exam-

ple of expository preaching at its best. Lloyd-Jones's analysis of carnality and spirituality is designed to expose the reason for the former and the way to acquire the latter. 227.1'07.L77 7:1-8:4

Newman, Barclay, and **Eugene Nida.** *A Translator's Handbook on Paul's Letter to the Romans.* New York: American Bible Society, 1973.

The syntax of this volume is of particular importance, and the authors attempt to resolve some of the problems inherent in the text. As with all volumes in this series, the thrust is to meet the needs of translators. Pastors and seminarians may also find these works helpful. 227.1'06:N46

Conzelmann, Hans. *I Corinthians: A Commentary on the First Epistle to the Corinthians.* Translated by James W. Leitch. Philadelphia: Fortress Press, 1975.

†Following a critical introduction which evades many of the matters presently the subject of debate, Conzelmann settles down to painstaking textual criticism. 227.2'07.C74

Schmithals, Walter. *Gnosticism in Corinth: An Investigation of the Letters to the Corinthians.* Translated by John E. Steely. Nashville: Abingdon Press, 1971.

†A critical treatment of the influence of the gnostics on the beliefs of those in Corinth. 273.1.S6

*Barrett, Charles Kingsley. *A Commentary on the Second Epistle to the Corinthians.* Harper's New Testament Commentaries. New York: Harper and Row, 1973.

†An exegetical study which will be of help to the expository preacher. 227.3'07.B27

DeWolf, Lotan Harold. *Galatians: A Letter for Today.* Grand Rapids: Wm. B. Eerdmans Publishing Co., 1971.

†The author's view of the inspiration and authority of the Scriptures is such that he regards the Bible as a "more or less accurate" human document. He does not deal with the historic setting which gave rise to the epistle and finds in its teaching the cure for many of America's contemporary ills. 227.4'06.D51

Drescher, John M. *Spirit Fruit.* Scottsdale, PA: Herald Press, 1975.

Preachers will welcome this full discussion of Galatians 5:22-23. It expounds, illustrates, and applies (with good stories and helpful anecdotes) Paul's teaching on the fruit of the Spirit. 242.D81

McDonald, Hugh Dermot. *Freedom in*

Faith. Old Tappan, NJ: Fleming H. Revell Co., 1974.

A concise, doctrinally helpful commentary. 227.4'07.M14

Barth, Markus. *The Anchor Bible: Ephesians.* 2 vols. Garden City, NY: Doubleday and Co., 1974.

†An extensive, critical exposition combining a careful blend of historical-grammatical exegesis with a down-to-earth application to the condition of the church today. A work of real quality which expository preachers will find most helpful. 227.5.B27

*Lloyd-Jones, David Martyn. *God's Way of Reconciliation: Studies in Ephesians 2.* Grand Rapids: Baker Book House, 1972.

A detailed exposition applying the truth of this passage to man's entire personality —mind, emotions, and will—and showing how, in Christ, God has made full provision for all of his needs. 227.5'07.L77 2

_____. *Life in the Spirit: In Marriage, Home and Work: An Exposition of Ephesians 5:18-6:9.* Grand Rapids: Baker Book House, 1975.

An invaluable discussion of the Biblical teaching on interpersonal relationships within the family and "on the job," with practical counsel for people in all walks of life. 227.5'07.L77 5:18-6:9

Lohse, Edward. *Colossians and Philemon: A Commentary on the Epistles to the Colossians and Philemon.* Translated by W. R. Poehlmann and R. J. Karris. Edited by H. Koester. Philadelphia: Fortress Press, 1971.

†Basing his approach to the text upon the latest critical data, the writer provides a wealth of information on the meaning of some Greek words and their usage. Good bibliographies. 227.7'07.L83

Martin, Ralph Philip. *Colossians: The Church's Lord and the Christian's Liberty.* Grand Rapids: Zondervan Publishing House, 1972.

A modern treatment which bridges the gap between a superficial study and a technical treatise. 227.7'07.M36

Thomas, William Henry Griffith. *Studies in Colossians and Philemon.* Grand Rapids: Baker Book House, 1973.

Based on the "notes" of this renowned expositor and theologian. Should serve to stimulate and encourage Bible teachers and pastors to engage in a vigorous expository ministry. 227.7.T36

Dibelius, Martin, and **Hans Conzelmann.**

The Pastoral Epistles. Translated by P. Buttolph and A. Yarbro. Edited by H. Koester. Philadelphia: Fortress Press, 1972.

A commentary built on the premise that these epistles are unauthentic, and that form-criticism is indispensable to exegesis. 227.83'06.D54

Best, Ernest. *A Commentary on the First and Second Epistles to the Thessalonians.* Harper's New Testament Commentaries. New York: Harper and Row, 1972.

†A critical, and in some respects, negative commentary. 227.81.B46

*Stott, John Robert Walmsey. *Guard the Gospel: The Message of II Timothy.* Downers Grove, IL: InterVarsity Press, 1973.

The first volume in a new series entitled *The Bible Speaks Today.* Deserves to be read by all who are interested in living dynamically for Christ in this present era. 227.84.57

Woychuk, Nicholas A. *Exposition of Second Timothy.* Old Tappan, NJ: Fleming H. Revell Co., 1974.

An original and creative exposition which abounds in illustrative material. 227.84'07.W91

General Epistles

Haas, C., M. De Jonge, and **J. L. Swellengrebel.** *A Translator's Handbook on the Letters of John.* New York: American Bible Society,

Can be of real use to expositors, and those whose Greek has become "rusty" will benefit from the translation hints and syntactical helps. 227.94'06.H11

*Lawlor, George Lawrence. *Translation and Exposition of the Epistle of Jude.* Nutley, NJ: Presbyterian and Reformed Publishing Co., 1972.

Includes a basic study of the original text. This treatment of Jude's letter is a most important one and deserves a place in the preacher's library. 227.97'07.L42

Revelation

Lindsey, Hal. *There's a New World Coming.* Santa Ana, CA: Vision House Publishers, 1973.

A popular exposition of the Revelation by the author of *The Late Great Planet Earth.* Premillennial. 228'07.L64

Phillips, John. *Exploring Revelation.* Chicago: Moody Press, 1974.

A careful commentary which those who preach through the Book of Revelation will want to consult. Premillennial. 228'07.P54

Apocrypha and Pseudepigrapha

Morris, Leon. *Apocalyptic.* Grand Rapids: Wm. B. Eerdmans Publishing Co., 1972.

A helpful introduction to apocalyptic literature showing its importance in Biblical study. 229.94.M83

Russell, David Syme. *The Method and Mes-*

sage of Jewish Apocalyptic. Philadelphia: Westminster Press, 1974.

First published in 1964. Makes an important contribution to our understanding of apocalyptic literature and enhances our knowledge of Judaistic beliefs in the intertestamental period. 229.913'06.R91

Chapter 4

DOCTRINAL THEOLOGY

*Chafer, Lewis Sperry. *Major Bible Themes*. Revised by John F. Walvoord. Grand Rapids: Zondervan Publishing House, 1974.

This manual of Christian doctrine retains in the revised edition the clarity and brevity for which the original was noted. Ideal for individual or adult study group use. 230'.51.C34M 1974

Furness, John Malcolm: *Vital Doctrines of*

the Faith. Grand Rapids: Wm. B. Eerdmans Publishing Co., 1974.

A brief but important presentation. 230.F98

*Ryrie, Charles Caldwell. *Survey of Bible Doctrine*. Chicago: Moody Press, 1972.

Writing with clarity and insight, the author discusses each aspect of doctrine in his unique and inimitable way. Ideal for discussion groups. 230.R99

Philosophy of Religion

Brown, Colin. *Philosophy and Christian Faith*. Downers Grove, IL: InterVarsity, 1969.

Introduces the main thinkers and schools of thought from the Middle Ages to the present day. The material is succinct and admirably serves the purpose for which the book was written. 201.B78

Diamond, Malcolm, Luria. *Contemporary Philosophy and Religious Thought*. New York: McGraw-Hill Book Co., 1974.

†A contemporary approach to the philosophy of religion with extensive discussions of Rudolph Otto, Martin Buber, Søren Kierkegaard, Rudolf Bultmann, and others. 200.1.D54

Geisler, Norman L. *Philosophy of Religion*. Grand Rapids: Zondervan Publishing House, 1974.

A Thomistic philosopher discusses God and experience, reason, language, and evil; and argues that while it is not logically necessary to believe in God, it is ontologically necessary to do so. 201.G27

Hudson, W. Donald. *A Philosophical Approach to Religion*. New York: Barnes and Noble, 1974.

This objective examination of the structure of religious belief treats among others the theories of Dietrich Bonhoeffer, Henry P. Van Dusen, Paul Van Buren, Paul Tillich, and Harvey Cox, and finds them deficient. 201.H86

Historical Theology

*Anderson, James Norman Dalrymple. *A Lawyer Among the Theologians*. Grand Rapids: Wm. B. Eerdmans Publishing Co., 1974.

A valuable critique of the higher-critical assumptions relating to the "historical Jesus," the atonement, and issues raised in Robinson's book, *The Difference in Being a*

Christian Today. 230.08.AN2

Bloesch, Donald G. *The Evangelical Renaissance.* Grand Rapids: Wm. B. Eerdmans Publishing Co., 1973.
†The author attempts to capitalize upon the evident signs of evangelical renewal and also to itemize some of the dangers. His stated purpose is to bring evangelicals and liberals closer together. The concessions he makes to those who do not hold conservative theological beliefs should be sufficient to warn evangelicals. 269.2.B62

*Conn, Harvie M. *Contemporary World Theology: A Layman's Guide.* Nutley, NJ: Presbyterian and Reformed Publishing Co., 1973.
Provides a clear and concise evangelical assessment of contemporary European theological movements. Includes a critical treatment of dispensationalism, fundamentalism, and neo-fundamentalism. Calvinistic. 230.09.C83

Danielou, Jean. *The Development of Christian Doctrine Before the Council of Nicaea.* In process. Philadelphia. Westminster Press, 1974.
Important studies which focus attention on the theology of Jewish Christianity and the reception given the gospel within Hellenism. Roman Catholic. 230.09.D22

Dictionary of Biblical Theology. 2d ed. rev. and enlarged. Edited by Xavier Leon-Dufour. New York: Seabury Press, 1973.
A widely used Roman Catholic reference work which concentrates on key words and important themes in the Bible. Forty new articles in this revision include Conscience, Cupidity, Predestination, Providence, Sexuality, and Yahweh. 230.03.D56L 1973

*Dollar, George W. *A History of Fundamentalism.* Greenville, SC: Bob Jones University Press, 1973.
This book surveys the history of Fundamentalism in America. While the author has only words of praise for militant Fundamentalists, and is unsparing in his censure of moderate and modified Fundamentalists, his contribution to American church history is very real. 230.09.F96.D69

Griffin, David R. *A Process Christology.* Philadelphia: Westminster Press, 1974.
†Standing in the tradition of Cobb, Ogden, Pettinger, and Williams, this book treats "process conceptuality" as a vehicle for the reconception and restatement of the Christian faith. 230.09.G87

Hamilton, Kenneth. *To Turn from Idols.*

Grand Rapids: Wm. B. Eerdmans Publishing Co., 1973.
A forthright analysis of the "cults" or "idols" of, for example, "relevance" and "change," which plague modern Christendom and detract from the reality of one's experience. 230.08.H18T

Harris, Horton. *David Frederick Strauss and His Theology.* Cambridge: At the University Press, 1973.
†Adequate attention is paid to Strauss's radical approach to the life of Christ and his advocacy of a desupernaturalized history of the human Jesus. Harris seeks to leave his readers with the impression that Strauss was right. 230'.0924.S8.H24

May, Rollo. *Paulus.* New York: Harper and Row, 1973.
A psychoanalytic evaluation of Paul Tillich. Nontheological and mostly sympathetic. 230'.0924.T46.M45

Meeks, M. Douglas. *Origins of the Theology of Hope.* Philadelphia: Fortress Press, 1974.
A full and sympathetic handling of Jürgen Moltmann's theology. 230'.0924.M73.M47

Moltmann, Jürgen. *The Crucified God: The Cross of Christ as the Foundation and Criticism of Christian Theology.* New York: Harper and Row, 1974.
†In the aftermath of his "theology of liberation," the author turns to Christology in a futile attempt to produce a "salvation" which will lead to a political liberation. 230'.0924.M73

Pelikan, Jaroslav. *The Christian Tradition: A History of the Development of Doctrine.* In process. Chicago: University of Chicago Press, 1972.
Scheduled for five volumes, these studies are valuable in acquiring a comprehensive grasp of the development of theological thought. 230.09.P36

Sheridan, John D. *The Hungry Sheep: Catholic Doctrine Restated Against Contemporary Attacks.* New Rochelle, NY: Arlington House, 1974.
A trenchant apologetic of the basic doctrines of Roman Catholicism. 230.2.SH5

Stone, Ronald H. *Reinhold Niebuhr: Prophet to Politicians.* Nashville: Abingdon Press, 1973.
While Stone does not deal with this neo-orthodox theologian's theology, he does describe his influence on society. Disciples of Niebuhr will welcome this treatise; others will

find that the writer's obvious sympathy with Niebuhr minimizes his objectivity. 230.0924.N55:S7

Thielicke, Helmut. *The Evangelical Faith, Vol. 1: Prolegamena; The Relation of Theology to Modern Thought Forms*. Translated and edited by Geoffrey W. Bromiley. Grand Rapids: William B. Eerdmans Publishing Co., 1974.

This translation of *Der evangelische Glaube* contains much that will cause concern to committed evangelicals. Thielicke, however, does offer some well-reasoned criticisms of modern existentialists and exposes the fallacies inherent in secularism. 230.09.T34 v.1

Welch, Claude. *Protestant Thought in the Nineteenth Century, 1799-1870*. New Haven: Yale University Press, 1972.

†The decline of Neo-orthodoxy is permitting the "theological grandsons" of liberalism to look at their grandfathers. This backward look is leading to a refurbishing of the reputations and contributions of men such as Schleirmacher, Ritschl, and Troeltsch. Welch's volume forms an enlightening survey of this era of history. 209'.034.W44

Hanson, Richard Patrick Crosland. *The Attractiveness of God: Essays in Christian Doctrine*. Richmond: John Knox Press, 1973.

†An attempt to establish Christian doctrine upon liberal theological hypotheses. 230.3'08.H19

The Godhead

God the Father

*France, R. T. *The Living God*. Downers Grove, IL: InterVarsity Press, 1973.

This popular study centers in what the Bible teaches about God and His dealings with men. 231.1.F84

Lightner, Robert Paul. *The First Fundamental: God*. Nashville: Thomas Nelson, 1973.

Beginning with a concise presentation of the historic arguments for the existence of God, the author then concentrates upon the heart of theology—the being and nature of God. The inclusion of charts enhances the usefulness of the book for general readers. 231.1.L62

Malik, Charles Habib. *The Wonder of Being*. Waco, TX: Word Books, 1974.

A penetrating examination of the cosmological argument by one who is philosophically and theologically competent to do so. 231'.042.M29

Ott, Heinrich. *God*. Philadelphia: Fortress Press, 1974.

†This study, by Karl Barth's successor at the University of Basel, seeks to provide a creditable rationale for the existential approaches of Buber and Tillich. Antitrinitarian. 231.0T8

*Packer, James Innell. *Knowing God*. Downers Grove, IL: InterVarsity Press, 1973.

These essays describe the kind of relationship redeemed man may enjoy with God—"a relationship calculated to thrill a man's heart." Part I deals with the blessings and benefits of knowing God; Part II with who God is; and Part III with the effect these truths should have on our lives. 231.P12

*Wenham, John William. *The Goodness of God*. Downers Grove, IL: InterVaristy Press, 1974.

This discussion of the problem of evil shows how the doctrine of Providence meshes with the severity and goodness of God. After developing a ninefold set of principles, Wenham applies these to different problem areas of faith and morality. The unique strengths of this book are marred by the writer's adherence to a "conditional immortality," and a relativism in ethics which makes some evils "necessary" and others "allowable." 231.8.W48

God the Holy Spirit

Carter, Charles Webb. *The Person and Ministry of the Holy Spirit: A Wesleyan Perspective*. Grand Rapids: Baker Book House, 1974.

A Biblical and evangelical study of considerable value even to those who do not subscribe to the author's Wesleyan-Holiness point of view. 231.2.C24

Fitch, William. *The Ministry of the Holy Spirit*. Grand Rapids: Zondervan Publishing House, 1974.

Geared to the needs of the individual and the congregational life of the church. Warns against a "unitarianism of the Son" to the neglect of the Spirit. Provides a helpful section on the gifts of the Spirit and a critique of Pentecostalism, past and present. Calvinistic. 231.3.F55

*Unger, Merrill Frederick. *The Baptism and Gifts of the Holy Spirit.* Chicago: Moody Press, 1974.

This revision of *The Baptizing of the Holy Spirit* updates the earlier material and provides a helpful guide in the midst of confusion over the charismatic movement. 231.3.UN3

Christology

Blaiklock, Edward Musgrave. *Who Was Jesus?* Chicago: Moody Press, 1974.

Presents the testimony of pagan writers to the historicity of Christ, and examines and refutes the theories of those who doubt His Messiahship. 232.09.B57

Bowker, John. *Jesus and the Pharisees.* Cambridge: At the University Press, 1973.

Briefly annotated translations of passages which shed light on the historical discussion of the Pharisees. Sources cited are Josephus, the Mishnah, Tosefta, and the Talmuds. For some of the material there is no other standard English version available. 232.9'5.B67

Brown, Raymond E. *The Virginal Conception and Bodily Resurrection of Jesus.* New York: Paulist Press, 1973.

†In dealing with the relation between history and dogma, Brown attempts to reconcile the world of the Bible student with the traditions of the Roman Catholic Church. He is an able and articulate form-critic and attempts a strange and difficult conjunction of two important themes. Of particular interest to those of his own communion. 232.921.B81

Christ and Spirit in the New Testament: Studies in Honour of Charles F. D. Moule. Edited by B. Lindars and S. S. Smalley. Cambridge: At the University Press, 1973.

This *Festschrift* contains twenty-seven essays by world-renowned scholars. Their reading will prove to be a mind-stretching experience even to those who do not agree with the viewpoints adopted by the contributors. 232.9.M86.C46

Conzelmann, Hans. *Jesus.* Translated by J. Raymond Lord. Edited by John Reumann. Philadelphia: Fortress Press, 1973.

†This material first appeared as an article in *Die Religion in Geschichte und Gegenwart* at the height of the "new quest" movement (which Conzelmann has since abandoned). Its

translation into English makes available to NT scholars a work otherwise relatively unknown in the United States. 232.908.C76

Bruce, Frederick Fyvie. *Jesus and Christian Origins Outside the New Testament.* Grand Rapids: Wm. B. Eerdmans Publishing Co., 1974.

Contains pertinent data from pagan sources—Josephus, the rabbis, the apocryphal gospels, Islam, and archaeology—relating to the person and work of Christ, and the origin of Christianity. 232.9'08.B83

*Chandler, Walter M. *The Trial of Jesus: From a Lawyer's Standpoint.* Atlanta, GA: Harrison Co., 1972.

First published in two volumes in 1908, this unabridged one-volume edition contains a lawyer's analysis and evaluation of Christ's Hebrew and Roman trials. 232.962.C36

Counts, William M. *Once a Carpenter.* Irvine, CA: Harvest House, 1975.

A contemporary and imaginative portrayal of events in the life of Christ. Of particular value in group discussions with young adults. 232.95.C83

Minear, Paul Sevier. *Commands of Christ: Authority and Implications.* Nashville: Abingdon Press, 1972.

†This scholarly volume draws attention to a subject frequently overlooked in NT scholarship. It considers the commands of Jesus rather than His assertions, invectives, or interrogations; claims that Christ's commands clearly point to His authority, and that they form the basis of salvation history. 232.9'54.M66

O'Collins, Gerald. *The Resurrection of Jesus Christ.* Valley Forge: Judson Press, 1973.

A concise summary of contemporary European theories relating to Christ's resurrection. While avoiding the extreme of skepticism, the writer fails to come out strongly in favor of the bodily resurrection of Jesus. Roman Catholic. 232.97.OC5

Robinson, John Arthur Thomas. *The Human Face of God.* Philadelphia: Westminster Press, 1973.

†This book is an example of what happens after a person has thrown off all submission to the authority of divine revelation. While some critics of contemporary theology regard this work as an autobiography of Robinson's struggles to date, others view it as an advanced form of apostasy. 232.R56

Schonfield, Hugh Joseph. *The Jesus Party.*

New York: Macmillan Co., 1974.

†Writing with greater reserve and paying more attention to historical data than was true in *The Passover Plot,* Schonfield attempts to analyze the Jewish-Christian group of the early church. He continues to brand them as revolutionary nationalists, and claims that they tried to make their message palatable to Gentiles by blaming the Jews for the crucifixion of Jesus. Highly speculative and anti-supernaturalistic. 209.SCH7

Schweizer, Eduard. *Jesus.* Translated by David E. Green. Philadelphia: John Knox Press, 1971.

†Based upon the 1968 German edition. Draws attention to the various perspectives on Jesus that find expression throughout the NT. Of particular significance is the chapter, "Jesus: The Man Who Fits No Formula." 232.9.SCH9

Sykes, S. W., and **J. P. Clayton.** *Christ, Faith and History: Cambridge Studies in Christology.* Cambridge: At the University Press, 1972.

†A learned collection of essays on the person and work of Christ, His origin, and place in history and theology. 232.S4

Anthropology, Soteriology

Barker, Harold. *Secure Forever.* Neptune, NJ: Loizeaux Brothers, 1974.

Surveys the teaching of the Bible on the subject of eternal security and then seeks to answer the criticisms leveled against the doctrine. 234.18.B24

Conscience, Contract, and Social Reality: Theory and Research in Behavioral Science. Edited by Ronald C. Johnson, Paul R. Dokecki, and O. Hobart Mowrer. New York: Holt, Rinehart and Winston, 1972.

Essays by social critics and psychologists providing an in-depth discussion of the relationship of the conscience to guilt, shame, crime, moral judgment, and more. 154.2.C74

*Fisk, Samuel. *Divine Sovereignty and Human Freedom.* Neptune, NJ: Loizeaux Brothers, 1973.

A forthright attempt to bring these complementary truths into focus, and to discuss the Biblical teaching supporting each view. Clarifies much of the confusion surrounding predestination and preterition. 233.7.F54

*Gromacki, Robert Glenn. *Salvation Is Forever.* Chicago: Moody Press, 1974.

A scholarly treatment relating the doctrine of eternal security to other facets of theology (e.g., sanctification, perserverance, etc.). Treats those passages of Scripture which seem to teach a contrary view with fairness and discernment. 234.18.G89

*Lee, Francis Nigel. *The Origin and Destiny of Man.* Nutley, NJ: Presbyterian and Reformed Publishing Co., 1974.

Five brief, Biblical lectures delivered at the inauguration of the Christian Studies Center, Memphis. Reformed. 233.L51

Maddi, Salvatore R. *Personality Theories: A Comparative Analysis.* Revised ed. Homewood, IL: Dorsey Press, 1972.

This secular approach to the study of the nature of man is of value for its evaluation of prevailing psychological theories. While Maddi does not support a Biblical view of man, his disenchantment with the theories of Freudians, behaviorists, and others, brings the reader to see the value of the Biblical model. 155.2.M26 1972

*Menninger, Karl. *Whatever Became of Sin?* New York: Hawthorn Books, 1973.

†The author is a psychiatrist, not a theologian, and as such, views sin existentially and is primarily concerned about its effect on human behavior. In spite of this perspective, he effectively traces the semantic game we have played with sin and calls on preachers to reassert their authority in exposing its many forms. 233.2.M52

Moltmann, Jürgen. *Man: Christian Anthropology in the Conflicts of the Present.* Philadelphia: Fortress Press, 1974.

†Whereas the author's ethical principles are of value, he is unable to deal adequately with the *imago Dei* because of his adherence to universalism and his unorthodox approach to the person and work of Christ. 233.M73

Tyrell, Francis Martin. *Man: Believer and Unbeliever.* Staten Island, NY: Alba House, 1974.

†A humanistic approach to anthropology. Attempts to retain the normative status of Christian revelation while adhering to principles totally at variance with the Biblical record. Roman Catholic. 234.T98

Yohn, Richard N. *Discover Your Spiritual Gift and Use It*. Wheaton: Tyndale House Publishers, 1974.

A timely and practical treatise on the development and use of gifts within the Body of Christ. Recommended for discussion groups. 234.1.Y7

Angelology

*Dickason, C. Fred. *Angels, Elect and Evil*. Chicago: Moody Press, 1975.

One of the most comprehensive discussions to appear to date. Of real value as a supplement to most systematic theologies. 235.3.D55

*Lindsey, Hal with **Carole C. Carlson.** *Satan Is Alive and Well on Planet Earth*. Grand Rapids: Zondervan Publishing House, 1972.

Following a dramatic first chapter, the writers settle down to analyzing the modern preoccupation with the occult and synthesizing the data they have gathered into a systematic treatment of Satanism. 235.47.L64

Tatford, Frederick A. *The Prince of Darkness*. Eastbourne, Sussex, Eng.: Prophetic Witness Publishing House, n.d.

A compact survey of Satan's rejection of God's right to rule and his struggle against His authority. Incidental light is shed on such subjects as the "sons of God" in Genesis 6 and the spiritual conflict in heavenly places. 235.47.T18

Eschatology

De Haan, Richard W. *Israel and the Nations in Prophecy*. Grand Rapids: Zondervan Publishing House, 1967.

Combines trends in the Middle East with a Biblical perspective on prophecy. 236.1.D36

Feinberg, Charles Lee, ed. *Jesus the King Is Coming*. Chicago: Moody Press, 1975.

In this symposium the writers tackle some important and difficult themes—all of which pertain to the role and responsibility of the church in the world at the present time. 236.F32

*Gundry, Robert H. *The Church and the Tribulation*. Grand Rapids: Zondervan Publishing House, 1973.

A vigorous and technical rejection of pretribulationalism by a NT scholar who is convinced of the posttribulationalism position. While weak in dealing with the material in the Gospels, Gundry places his emphasis on data from the Epistles. This book will become one of the main supports of posttribulationalism. 236.4.G95

Harkness, Georgia Elma. *Understanding the Kingdom of God*. Nashville: Abingdon Press, 1974.

Aiming at providing an understanding of the personal and social relevance of the Kingdom, this work focuses attention on new movements and the growth of conservative churches. Lacking in evangelical emphasis. 231.7.H22

Ladd, George Eldon. *The Presence of the Future*. Grand Rapids: Wm. B. Eerdmans Publishing Co., 1974.

A revision of *Jesus and the Kingdom*. In contrast to the former work which was mildly premillennial, there is nothing in this revision which would prevent Ladd being classified as amillennarian. 236.L12P

McCall, Thomas S., and **Zola Levitt.** *Satan in the Sanctuary*. Chicago: Moody Press, 1973.

A popular book dealing with the events which the authors believe are leading up to the Tribulation. 220.15.M12

MacPherson, David. *The Unbelievable Pretrib Origin*. Kansas City, MO: Heart of America Bible Study, 1973.

A valiant, though abortive, attempt to disprove pretribulationalism by claiming that the whole movement began with a Margaret MacDonald who received the doctrine through special revelation. This proposal lacks documentation. 236.4.M24

*Mason, Clarence E., Jr. *Prophetic Problems, with Alternate Solutions*. Chicago: Moody Press, 1973.

The writer has long been recognized for his ability to break out of traditional molds and do his own thinking. An original contribution on a variety of important eschatological themes. 236.M37

Payne, J. Barton. *Encyclopedia of Biblical Prophecy*. New York: Harper and Row, 1973.

Of value for its introduction to the interpretation of prophecy, but disappointing in that the author fails to apply some of these principles to the passages he discusses, and overlooks several important prophetic chapters in the Bible. 236.03.P29

*Price, Walter K. *The Coming Antichrist*. Chicago: Moody Press, 1974.

A comprehensive Biblical and historical study of the doctrine of the Antichrist. 236.P93

Reese, Alexander. *The Approaching Advent of Christ*. Grand Rapids: Grand Rapids International Publications, 1975.

Long out of print and difficult to procure, this work has now been made available again.

It embodies a critical examination of the teachings of J. N. Darby by an ardent post-tribulationist. 236.4.R25 1975

*Tan, Paul Lee. *The Interpretation of Prophecy*. Winona Lake, IN: Brethren Missionary Herald Books, 1974.

A cogent argument for the literal method of interpreting prophecy which satisfactorily grapples with the problems. 236'.06.T15

Walvoord, John Flipse and John Edward Walvoord. *Armageddon: Oil and the Middle East Crisis*. Grand Rapids: Zondervan Publishing House, 1974.

A candid explanation of Middle East tensions in the light of Biblical prophecy. Premillennial. 236.5.W17

Wood, Leon James. *The Bible and Future Events: An Introductory Survey of Last-Day Events*. Grand Rapids: Zondervan Publishing House, 1973.

An overview of God's prophetic program. Significant because it deals with eschatology from the viewpoint of a Semitic scholar. Provides an entirely new perspective on many old, timeworn themes. Premillennial. 236.W81

Future State

Winter, David. *Hereafter: What Happens After Death*. Wheaton: Harold Shaw Publishers, 1973.

A brief, Scriptually based book which draws on paranormal research to show the reasonableness of the Christian belief in life after death and the expectation of a bodily resurrection. Worthy of serious considera-

tion. 237.1.W68

Wolff, Richard. *The Last Enemy*. Grand Rapids: Baker Book House, 1974.

A survey of different attitudes toward death showing that only in Christianity can there be any certainty of a *blessed* future state. 237.1.W83

Creeds

*Kelly, John Norman Davidson. *Early Christian Creeds*. 3d ed. New York: David McKay Co., 1972.

Ably surveys the rise, development, and use of credal formuli. 238.1.K28

Pink, Arthur Walkington. *The Divine Covenants*. Grand Rapids: Baker Book House, 1973.

Omitting "the New Covenant," Pink discusses the other covenants from a strongly Reformed point of view. 238.P65

Sproul, Robert Charles. *The Symbol: An Exposition of the Apostle's Creed*. Nutley, NJ: Presbyterian and Reformed Publishing Co., 1973.

An evangelical exposition. 238.11.S7

Apologetics

*McDowell, Josh. *Evidence That Demands a Verdict*. Arrowhead Springs, CA: Campus Crusade for Christ, 1972.

Despite its lack of philosophical orienta-

tion, this book ranks with the best on the subject of Christian evidences. Ideal for use in high school or college groups. 239.M14

*Morris, Henry Madison. *Many Infallible Proofs*. San Diego: Creation-Life Publishers, 1974.

Building upon Christianity's historic reliability, the author develops a strong case for supernaturalism. He combines his mastery of scientific data with a careful evaluation of the Biblical material. An important work on Christian evidences. 239.M83

Sproul, Robert Charles. *The Psychology of Atheism*. Minneapolis: Bethany Fellowship, 1974.

A powerful apolegetic for a Biblical faith which answers the charge that a Christian's belief is motivated by his psychological needs, and shows that an atheist's "faith" is a direct result of his unwillingness to submit to the claims of Christ. 239.7.S7

Chapter 5

DEVOTIONAL LITERATURE

Christian Ethics

Cline, Victor B., ed. *Where Do You Draw the Line? An Exploration into Media Violence, Pornography, and Censorship.* Provo, UT: Brigham Young University Press, 1974.

An important book which explores, in a scientific manner, many areas of current concern long regarded by purveyors of liberal ethics as impossible to scrutinize. 363.31.C61

Cupitt, Don. *Crisis of Moral Authority: The Dethronement of Christianity.* London: Lutterworth Press, 1972.

†The author's vast learning is lost through his advocacy of a left-wing position and his scathing denunciation of the historical church's failure to keep pace with the moral "advance" of free-thinkers. He does nothing to point a way out of the present malaise and his excoriating remarks can only humiliate those who are already painfully aware of the problems. 241.04'03.C92

Drew, Donald J. *Images of Man: a Critique of the Contemporary Cinema.* Downers Grove, IL: Inter-Varsity Press, 1974.

A devastating exposé of the darkness of the cinematic jungle and the way in which movies have altered our cultural values. 301.16.D82

Fletcher, Joseph. *The Ethics of Genetic Control: Ending Reproductive Roulette.* Garden City, NY: Doubleday and Co., 1974.

†Pushes situational ethics to new extremes and shows again the depths to which a person may sink after abandoning belief in God's authoritative revelation. 176.F63E

Gardner, Reginald Frank Robert. *Abortion: The Personal Dilemma.* Grand Rapids: Wm. B. Eerdmans Publishing Co., 1972.

Of importance to all engaged in counseling ministries. Tackles openly and honestly the many and varied aspects of abortion. Recommended reading. 301.G17

Hamilton, Michael, ed. *The New Genetics and the Future of Man.* Grand Rapids: Wm. B. Eerdmans Publishing Co., 1972.

Concentrating on the ramifications of genetic engineering (for instance, artificial insemination), the contributors discuss "New Beginnings in Life," "Genetic Therapy," and "Pollution and Health." Kass, Ramsey, and Epstein present well-reasoned papers calling for caution. The other contributors represent a more "left-wing" approach, and their essays demand critical evaluation. 575.1.H18

Klotz, John William. *A Christian View of Abortion.* St. Louis: Concordia Publishing House, 1973.

A candid discussion of the issues and alternatives to abortion. Judicious and conservative. 241.697.K69

Pannenberg, Wolfhart. *The Idea of God and Human Freedom.* Translated by R. A. Wilson. Philadelphia: Westminster Press, 1973.

†Continuing the train of thought begun in *Basic Issues in Theology,* Pannenberg opposes Bultmann's approach to the NT. He draws heavily upon form-criticism and painstakingly probes into texts referring to the Spirit of God. The book lacks real cohesion and has value mainly for scholars interested in keeping abreast of the latest European thought. 201'.1.P19

*Rushdoony, Rousas J. *The Politics of Pornography.* New York: Arlington House, 1974.

A detailed exposé of pornography with important chapters on such matters as its history and legal battles. Probes the foundations of the problem and shows why it has grown to such proportions. Includes an examination of the underlying philosophical presuppositions, the pagan origin of the movement, and the violence which it fosters. 301.21.R89

Vincent, Merville O. *God, Sex and You.* Philadelphia: A. J. Holman Co., 1971.

Grapples with the problems of permissiveness, exposes the fallacies of the "Playboy" philosophy, and seeks to liberate sex from the legalism which surrounds it in many Christian communities. Provides practical counsel for both single and married people. A wholesome, objective treatment of a difficult subject. 301.41.V74

Christian Living

Bloesch, Donald G. *Wellsprings of Renewal: Promise in Christian Community Life.* Grand Rapids: Wm. B. Eerdmans Publishing Co., 1973.
†An historical and theological analysis of community life in Protestantism. Traces the various movements within the evangelical tradition. Reflects the author's doctrinal drift through his adherence to a broadly ecumenical theology. 255.8.B.62

Christenson, Laurence. *The Renewed Mind.* Minneapolis: Bethany Fellowship, 1974.
Basing his study squarely on the Scriptures, Christenson shows us how to bridge the gap between what we are and what God intended us to be. 248.4.C46

Collins, Gary R. *The Christian Psychology of Paul Tournier.* Grand Rapids: Baker Book House, 1973.
This work provides a summary of Tournier's ideas. Particularly helpful when viewed in the light of Tournier's own theological commitments. 248'.0924.T64.C69

***Douty, Norman F.** *Union with Christ.* Swengel, PA: Reiner Publications, 1973.
Written by an evangelical who is well grounded in theology, this study of one of the central themes of the NT deserves careful reading by all who wish to know more of God's provision for them in Christ. 248:4.D74

Elliott, Neil. *The Gods of Life.* New York: Macmillan Co., 1974.
Deals with the same subject matter as Maguire's *Death by Choice.* Discusses limited euthanasia and presents a strong case for death with dignity, unencumbered by devices which only delay the inevitable. 174.24.EL5

Fromm, Erich. *The Anatomy of Human Destructiveness.* New York: Holt, Rinehart and Winston, 1973.
†The writer's "self-help" books continue to provide readers with a nontechnical, heuristic approach to self-understanding. Fromm affirms the possibility of self-actualization over against the pessimistic prognosis of some Freudians. His practical counsel exposes the cause of violence, and his keen sense of the American character makes his writings relevant to our generation. Preachers will find his analysis of the human situation insightful. 152.5.F91

***Hoekema, Anthony A.** *The Christian Looks at Himself.* Grand Rapids: Wm. B. Eerdmans Publishing Co., 1975.
The author is well able to apply psychological and theological concepts to the study of the nature of man and the problem of his self-esteem. While some readers will object to his handling of Romans 7, the fact remains that Hoekema has made an invaluable contribution to the study of the *imago Dei.* 248.4.H67

Jabay, Earl. *The God-Players.* Grand Rapids: Zondervan Publishing House, 1970.
Shows the inherent ugliness of a self-controlled life and prescribes the only cure—a life given over to God and lived under the control of the Holy Spirit. An important work! 248.4.J11

Landorf, Joyce. *Mourning Song.* Old Tappan, NJ: Fleming H. Revell Co., 1974.
A deeply human story of personal loss showing the emotional reaction to the inevitability of death—denial, anger, bargaining, depression, and finally acceptance—and how God restores our spirits and ministers comfort to troubled hearts. 248.86.L23

Mallory, James D. *The Kink and I.* Wheaton: Victor Books, 1973.

A valiant attempt to integrate psychological principles with a Biblical way of life. Revealing and rewarding reading. 248.4.M29

May, Rollo. *Power and Innocence: A Search for the Sources of Violence.* New York: W. W. Norton, 1972.

This sequel to *Love and Will* shows how power, in balance, is the effective foundation for love. Also points out how the absence of that balance leads to the abuse of power and this, in turn, results in different forms of violence. 301.6'33.M44

Middelmann, Udo. *Pro-existence.* Downers Grove. IL: Inter-Varsity Press, 1974.

An associate of Francis Schaeffer deals objectively with such topics as creativity, work, property, and selfishness. His analysis of the contemporary scene forms the basis of his eloquent plea to return to Christlike living. 248.4.M58

Pink, Arthur Walkington. *Spiritual Growth: Growth in Grace, or Christian Progress.* Grand Rapids: Baker Book House, 1972.

A "meaty" volume dealing not only with many timeless truths but some surprises as well. As with all of Pink's works, this one needs to be studied. 248.4.P65

*Schaeffer, Edith. *Hidden Art.* Wheaton: Tyndale House Publishers, 1971.

Believing that Christians should be more rather than less creative than non-Christians, the wife of Francis Schaeffer shows how we may attain to some degree of God's creativity. 246.SCH1

Smith, John E. *The Analogy of Experience: An Approach to Understanding Religious Truth.* New York: Harper and Row, 1973.

Comprising the Warfield Lectures, Princeton Theological Seminary, 1970, these philosophically oriented studies probe the centrality of experience in the Christian faith. 201.S6

*Stott, John Robert Walmsey. *Your Mind Matters: The Place of the Mind in the Christian Life.* Downers Grove, IL: InterVarsity Press, 1972.

A brilliant treatise emphasizing the place and importance of proper cognitive development in the life and experience of every believer. 248.4.S7

*Wagner, Maurice E. *Put It All Together: Developing Inner Security.* Grand Rapids: Zondervan Publishing House, 1974.

A masterful blending of psychology and theology showing their application to the damaged self-concept and poor interpersonal relations of many Christians. 248.4.W12

Christian Home

Adams, Jay Edward. *Christian Living in the Home.* Nutley, NJ: Presbyterian and Reformed Publishing Co., 1972.

Applies the teaching of the Bible to the dilemma facing Christians as they establish their own homes. Recommended! 249.AD1

Andelin, Aubrey P. *Man of Steel and Velvet.* Santa Barbara, CA: Pacific Press, 1973.

The counterpart of the *Fascinating Woman* contains some dos and don'ts for men which, if followed, will make for happier homes, more secure wives, and a healthier environment for children. 301.411.AN2M

Andrews, Gini. *Your Half of the Apple.* Grand Rapids: Zondervan Publishing House, 1972.

A realistic treatment of the problems as well as the opportunities facing single people in a couple's world. 248.843.AN2

Augsburger, David W. *Cherishable: Love and Marriage.* Scottsdale, PA: Herald Press, 1973.

This book has a variety of uses. One of them is with discussion groups. It may also serve as a guide for any couple interested in developing creative marital relationships. 249.AU4

Berger, Evelyn Miller. *Triangle: The Betrayed Wife.* Chicago: Nelson-Hall Co., n.d.

Infidelity has become commonplace in our society, but what emotional effect does it have on those who are "cheated"? This book exposes the causes leading up to extramarital relations. While secular, and tending to exonerate the wife from culpability, this treatment nevertheless contains an abundance of sane counsel. 301.415.B45

Bricklin, Barry, and **Patricia M. Bricklin.** *Strong Family, Strong Child: The Art of*

Working Together to Develop a Healthy Child. New York: Delacorte Press, 1970.

By combining their skills as psychologists and their experience as parents, the authors provide valuable counsel and practical guidelines for rearing children. 301.43.B76

Dobson, James C. *Hide or Seek*. Old Tappan, NJ: Fleming H. Revell Co., 1974.

By the author of *Dare to Discipline*. Contains numerous practical suggestions for building a child's self-esteem. Blends the teaching of the Bible with sound psychological principles. 301.43.D65 (Alt. DDC.649.1019)

Ellul, Jacques. *Hope in Time of Abandonment*. Translated by C. Edward Hopkin. New York: Seabury Press, 1973.

Written with conviction and insight. Deals with a host of false hopes common to our age. Warns against a false optimism and urges readers to place their confidence solely in God's loving kindness and providence. 234.2.EL5

Evening, Margaret. *Who Walk Alone: A Consideration of the Single Life*. Downers Grove, IL: InterVarsity Press, 1974.

A bold attempt to come to grips with singleness, particularly among those in their twenties. Deals factually with the matter of sexuality, the risks of love, and the dilemma of loneliness. Can be read with profit by the widowed and divorced as well. 248.843.EV2

Florio, Anthony. *Two to Get Ready*. Old Tappan, NJ: Fleming H. Revel Co., 1974.

A basic, readable guide to emotional maturity designed for those contemplating marriage. Of inestimable use to pastors and those who counsel would-be-weds in that it lays down Biblical principles for a lifetime of commitment to Christ and to each other. 301.414.F65

Gleason, John J., Jr. *Growing Up to God: Eight Steps in Religious Development*. Nashville: Abingdon Press, 1975.

Survey of religious development—from birth to death. Builds on the psychology of Eric Erikson and attempts to integrate human psychology with theology. Stimulating. 220'.19.G47

*Hendricks, Howard George. *Heaven Help the Home*. Wheaton: Victor Books, 1973.

A candid and refreshing analysis of the pressures brought to bear on homemakers . . . and what they may do about them. Valuable for newlyweds. 248.8.H38

Hodge, Marshall B. *Your Fear of Love*. Garden City, NY: Doubleday and Co., 1967.

Many people are unable to form any close relationships with others because they are unconsciously afraid of *love*. This book explains the reasons why this occurs and how they may be overcome. 152.4'42.H66

Kaye, Evelyn. *The Family Guide to Children's Television*. New York: Random House, 1974.

While written from a non-Christian perspective, this book presents an aspect of child-rearing of which every parent should be aware. Brief evaluations of most current TV shows are included. 791.455.K18

Mace, David Robert and **Vera Mace.** *We Can Have Better Marriages If We Really Want Them*. Nashville: Abingdon Press, 1974.

One of the better books to be published on the subject in recent years. Focuses attention on the causes of contention, the way in which difficulties may be resolved, and the best means for achieving lasting enrichment. 301.42.M15

*McDonald, Cleveland. *Creating a Successful Christian Marriage*. Grand Rapids: Baker Book House, 1975.

Not since Small's *Design for Christian Marriage* has anything as comprehensive and readable been attempted. McDonald shows himself to be abreast of the latest trends and ably integrates psychological and sociological concepts with the Scriptures to form a Biblical basis for a successful, maturing relationship. 301.42.M14

McGinnis, Marilyn. *Single*. Old Tappan, NJ: Fleming H. Revell Co., 1974.

A clear, positive assessment of the qualities that make the difference between the lonely, self-pitying, bitter, and depressed single young adult, and those who live happy, meaningful lives. Should be in every church library! 248.843.M17

Masters, William H. and **Virginia E. Masters (Johnson).** *The Pleasure Bond: A New Look at Sexuality and Commitment*. Boston: Little, Brown and Co., 1975.

Answers many questions that have long plagued married couples and marriage counselors. One of its strengths lies in the new emphasis the authors place on loyalty to one's marriage partner as the only basis of proper communication and satisfactory intimacy 301.41'7.M39

*Narramore, Stanley Bruce.** An Ounce of Prevention: A Parent's Guide to Moral and Spiritual Growth of Children.* Grand Rapids: Zondervan Publishing House, 1973.

Well illustrated with line drawings by Diane Head, this handy volume lays down sound principles for the purposeful, planned development of a child's moral sensibilities. Questions are included to help parents work through problem areas. 649.7.N16

Richards, Lawrence O. *You, the Parent.* Chicago: Moody Press, 1974.

A provocative "how to" manual describing the principles of parenting and the dynamics of parent-child relationships. 301.42.R39

Rogers, Carl Ransom. *Becoming Partners: Marriage and Its Alternatives.* New York: Delacorte Press, 1972.

In an era of "liberation" and new life-styles with many preferring to live together without undergoing the formality of marriage, this critique of the personality changes of those who struggle to "become partners" is most revealing. While secular in its approach, there is a great deal in this book which tacitly confirms the superiority of the Biblical model. 301.42.R63

Shafner, Evelyn. *When Mothers Work.* Santa Barbara, CA: Pacific Press, 1972.

A perceptive, practical treatment of an issue which can cause serious problems in today's milieu. 301.427.SH1

*Small, Dwight Hervey.** Christian: Celebrate Your Sexuality.* Old Tappan, NJ: flem-ing H. Revell Co., 1974.

Grounded in the historic tradition of the Judeo-Christian ethic, this book explains sex as being, first and foremost, God's idea and His gift to mankind. Judicious. 241.6'6.S1

*Strauss, Richard L.** Marriage Is for Love.* Wheaton: Tyndale House Publishers, 1973.

These thirteen chapters cover almost every facet of marriage, are grounded in the Scriptures, and make this small volume ideal for adult discussion groups. 248.8.S8

*Strommen, Merton.** Five Cries of Youth.* New York: Harper and Row, 1974.

Based upon data from extensive questionnaires completed by young people, this book tabulates their most urgent needs. 170.202.S8

Tournier, Paul. *Learn to Grow Old.* Translated by Edwin Hudson. New York: Harper and Row, 1974.

"Prepare early for retirement," is this author's advice, not with a view to relaxing in the sun, but of preparing for a different role —that of injecting an atmosphere of greater humanity into society. 301.43'5.T64

Wagemaker, Herbert. *Why Can't I Understand My Kids?* Grand Rapids: Zondervan Publishing House, 1973.

These short chapters aim at providing guidelines which will help parents bridge the generation gap. 301.42'7.W12

*Wright, H. Norman.** Communication: Key to Your Marriage.* Glendale, CA: Regal Books, 1974.

An important book on marital counseling showing from the Scriptures how husbands and wives may improve their marriages through proper communication. 261.8'34'27.W93

Chapter 6

PASTORAL THEOLOGY

Preaching Homiletics

Demaray, Donald E. *An Introduction to Homiletics*. Grand Rapids: Baker Book House, 1974.

This clear delineation between didactic and kerygmatic preaching contains numerous practical suggestions for sermon building. 251.D39

*Neil, William (comp.). *Concise Dictionary of Religious Quotations*. Grand Rapids: Wm. B. Eerdmans Publishing Co., 1974.

Of tremendous value to preachers and writers. Arranged alphabetically by topic. 808.8.N31

Schaeffer, Francis August. *No Little People*. Downers Grove, IL: InterVarsity Press, 1974.

Extols the virtues of several men of the Bible and emphasizes the uniqueness of their position in the history of redemption. 252.5.SCH1N

Stewart, James Stuart. *The River of Life*. Nashville: Abingdon Press, 1972.

Seventeen practical, penetrating messages showing the all-sufficient provision of God for daily living. 253.5.S4

Turnbull, Ralph G. *A History of Preaching*. Vol. 3. Grand Rapids: Baker Book House, 1974.

The publication of this work brings up to date Edwin Dargan's monumental contribution. 251'.009.D24T

Williams, Duncan. *Trousered Apes: Sick Literature in a Sick Society*. New Rochelle, NY: Arlington House, 1972.

A provocative treatise on the various forms of pornography in our society, the multi-million dollar industry it supports, and the "commentary" it provides on our social and cultural values. Pastors will find an abundance of illustrative material between the covers of this book. Recommended. 809'933'53.W67

*Wirt, Sherwood Eliot and **Kersten Beckstrom (comp.).** *Living Quotations for Christians*. New York: Harper and Row, 1974.

Arranged in alphabetical order by subject with author and topic indexes, this volume will be of real value to preachers. 808.8.W73

Pastoral Duties, Pastoral Life

Albers, Henry. *Principles of Management: A Modern Approach*. New York: John Wiley and Sons, 1974.

An assessment of the problems and pressures facing executives in all walks of life. 658.4.AL1 1974

Bormann, Ernest G., and **Nancy C. Bor-**mann. *Effective Committees and Groups in the Church*. Minneapolis: Augsburg Publishing Co., 1973.

Points the way to committee effectiveness through an understanding of the various roles in the group process. 301.14.B64

Blumenfeld, Samuel L. *How to Start Your*

Own Private School–And Why You Should.
New Rochelle, NY: Arlington House, 1972.

In this penetrating critique of the inadequacies of public schooling the author presents reasons for Christian businessmen to start private schools. The comments on fund raising are particularly appropriate.
371.02'0973.B66

Coulson, William. *Groups, Gimmicks, and Instant Gurus.* New York: Harper and Row, 1973.

This provocative work explores the values and weaknesses of encounter groups. It restores a much-needed balance to group therapy—a balance largely lost in the present-day proliferation of techniques. 301.11.C83

Demaray, Donald E. *Preacher Aflame.* Grand Rapids: Baker Book House, 1972.

A brief statement of the excitement which accompanies a preacher's realization of his high calling. Particularly valuable for seminarians. 253.2.D39

*Drucher, Peter Ferdinand. *Management: Tasks, Responsibilities, Practices.* New York: Harper and Row, 1973.

Pastors who have benefited from Drucker's practical treatises on the development of management and executive skills will welcome his *magnum opus.* 658.4.D84

Dubin, Robert. *Human Relations in Administration.* 4th ed. Englewood Cliffs: Prentice-Hall, 1973.

An extremely valuable work for those who are called upon to pastor large churches. 658.4.D85 1973

Ellens, J. Harold. *Models of Religious Broadcasting.* Grand Rapids: Wm. B. Eerdmans Publishing Co., 1974.

In an era of mass media communications, this book ranks as one of the most important works on the subject. 253.7'8.EL5

*Gillaspie, Gerald Whiteman. *The Restless Pastor.* Chicago: Moody Press, 1974.

This practical book deals honestly and objectively with a problem nearly every pastor faces at one time or another: "Should I remain where I am, or move to another pastorate?" Among the aspects not dealt with by Gillaspie are the average cost of living in a new area, schools for children, and where to buy a home. Information about these vital issues has been handled in *The Minister's Library,* pp. 254-55. 253.2.G41

Gilmore, Alec. *Tomorrow's Pulpit.* Valley Forge: Judson Press, 1975.

Comprising the Edwin Stephen Griffith Memorial Lectures on Preaching, Cardiff Baptist College, Wales, 1973, these lectures assess the task of the ministry in the light of the needs of the closing decades of this era. 251.G42

Griffith, Leonard. *We Have This Ministry.* Waco, TX: Word Books, 1974.

Drawing upon a wealth of practical pastoral experience on both sides of the Atlantic, Griffith challenges and counsels his colleagues to be true to their mission as ministers of God. 253.G87

Hendrix, Olan. *Management and the Christian Worker.* Ft. Washington, PA: Christian Literature Crusade, 1974.

An important work for those in the ministry who wish to know how to make better, more productive use of their time. 254.H38

Holck, Manfred. *Making It on a Pastor's Pay.* Nashville: Abingdon Press, 1974.

A practical treatise. 253.2.H69 (Alt. DDC 332.024)

Jackson, Benjamin Franklin, Jr., ed. *You and Communication in the Church: Skills and Techniques.* Waco, TX: Word Books, 1974.

Emphasizing the need for effective communication—written, visual, and spoken—the writers show how the necessary skills may be developed and used. 001.54.J13

MacDonald, Charles R. *Administration of the Work of the Local Church.* Minneapolis: Central Seminary Press, 1973.

A brief, practical treatise designed for those who lack administrative expertise. 254.M14

*Nordland, Frances. *The Unprivate Life of a Pastor's Wife.* Chicago: Moody Press, 1972.

Candid reflections on the trials and joys of those who accompany their husbands into the pastoral ministry. 253.22.N75

Rouch, Mark A. *Competent Ministry: A Guide to Effective Continuing Education.* Nashville: Abingdon Press, 1974.

Sage counsel for those in the ministry as well as those preparing for it. Should be read by laymen on church boards as well. 207'.1.R75

Schul, William D. *How to Be an Effective Group Leader.* Chicago: Nelson-Hall, 1975.

Pastors who are looking for an easy-to-read, down-to-earth manual on the techniques of effective group work will find their answer in this handy book. 301.15.SCH8

Schuller, Robert Harold. *Your Church Has*

Real Possibilities! Glendale, CA: Regal Books, 1975.

A presentation of the church growth principles which the author has used in his Institute for Successful Leadership. 254'.008.SCH9

*Smith, Wilbur Moorehead. *The Minister in His Study.* Chicago: Moody Press, 1973.

Based upon lectures delivered at the Trinity Evangelical Divinity School, Illinois. Highlights the importance of the pastor's *sanctum sanctorum.* 253.S6

Søgaard, Viggo B. *Everything You Need to Know for a Cassette Ministry.* Minneapolis: Bethany Fellowship, 1974.

An important handbook dealing with the place and importance of cassette tapes in the total program of the local church. 266'.0028.S2

Stewart, Charles William. *Person and Profession: Career Development in the Ministry.* Nashville: Abingdon Press, 1974.

Designed to focus attention on the pastor's humanness. Also shows him how to make the necessary adjustments so that he will be able to survive the pressures of the times. 253.2.S4

*Stogdill, Ralph M. *Handbook of Leadership.* New York: The Free Press, 1974.

Based upon more that forty years of research into the subject of leadership. Deserves to be read repeatedly by all who are engaged in maintaining stability in a world of change and guiding others toward a meaningful future. 158.4.S6

Sudgen, Howard F., and Warren W. Wiersbe. *When Pastors Wonder How.* Chicago: Moody Press, 1973.

Arranged in question-and-answer format, these veteran pastors share their experiences with others in the ministry. Valuable for those preparing for the pastorate. 253.S3

Towns, Elmer L. *Have the Public Schools Had It?* Nashville: Thomas Nelson and Sons, 1974.

Packed with startling comments about the violence, lack of discipline, and ineffective teaching in our public schools. Provides guidelines on what concerned citizens may do about this. Buy it and read it. 371.01'0973.T66

Truman, Ruth. *Underground Manual for Ministers' Wives.* Nashville: Abingdon Press, 1974.

Directs attention to the practical needs of pastors' wives, and the brides of seminarians. Discusses such relevant subjects as sex, other women, caring for children, and maintaining one's own spiritual life. Helpful. 253.22.T77

Wheeler, Richard. *Pagans in the Pulpit.* New Rochelle, NY: Arlington House, 1974.

With moderate evangelicals producing a massive amount of literature on the need for Christians to become involved in social action, it is refreshing to find someone who states unequivocally that the need of the church is for priorities with individual salvation high on the list. 261.8.W57

Pastoral Counseling

Adams, Jay Edward. *Shepherding God's Flock.* Nutley, NJ: Presbyterian and Reformed Publishing Co., 1974.

In this volume the popular author of *Competent to Counsel* draws attention to the pastor's personal life and his ministry of visitation. 253.5.AD1

———. *Competent to Counsel.* Nutley, NJ: Presbyterian and Reformed Publishing Co., 1970.

This book "took the Christian world by storm." Its strengths are obvious; what are regarded as its weaknesses are not as readily discernable. The author traces all personality problems to sin, and his advocacy of a *nouthetic* (rather that a *paracletic*) model of counseling is widely regarded as being too restrictive. 253.5.AD1

Biblical and Psychological Perspectives for Christian Counselors. Edited by Robert K. Bower. South Pasadena, CA: Publishers Services, William Carey Library, 1974.

A pioneer work of considerable merit. 253.5.B47

Clinebell, Howard John, Jr. *The People Dynamic: Changing Self and Society Through Growth Groups.* New York: Harper and Row, 1972.

Having pioneered a "formula" for personal growth, and having tested his theory in clinical settings, the author makes available to a wide readership the strategies he has used with good success. 301.11'3.C61

Collins, Gary R. *Fractured Personalities.* Carol Stream, IL: Creation House, 1972.

Writing for laymen, Collins discusses abnormal psychology. His diagnosis and suggestions for treatment are based upon the Scriptures. 157.C69

Crook, Roger H. *An Open Book to the Christian Divorcee.* Nashville: Broadman Press, 1974.
After arguing that divorce should be a "last resort," the author deals with a variety of problems which may lead up to divorce. He discusses the ways a transition from married to single life can be made and calls for maturity on the part of both parties. A compassionate treatment. 301.42'84.C87

Hudson, Robert Lofton. *Til Divorce Do Us Part.* Nashville: T. Nelson & Sons, 1973.
There is much to learn about compassion in this book, but it is to be regretted that the heart-wrenching experiences of his clients has colored the writer's approach to the Scriptures. He sets aside the normal understanding of Biblical passages dealing with divorce as literalistic and an impediment to counseling, and adopts instead a permissive stance by concluding that the Bible permits divorce and remarriage *for believers* on grounds other than infidelity. 301.4284.H86

Justice, William G. *Don't Sit on the Bed.* Nashville: Broadman Press, 1973.
Brief, pointed chapters describing the "dos" and "don'ts" of visiting the sick. 253.5.J98

McLemore, Clinton. *Clergyman's Psychological Handbook.* Grand Rapids:

Wm. B. Eerdmans Publishing Co., 1974.
This summary of the major functional and organic disorders pastors encounter in their counseling ministry is of particular value in determining when to refer someone to a psychologist, or a psychiatrist. 253.5.M22

Troup, Stanley B., and **William A. Greene, eds.** *The Patient, Death, and the Family.* New York: Charles Scribner's Sons, 1974.
Of particular value to those engaged in counseling. The contributors discuss death from nearly every point of view. Missing, however, is a theological perspective. 301.428'6.T75

Wilke, Richard B. *The Pastor and Marriage Group Counseling.* Nashville: Abingdon Press, 1974.
An important book outlining some new techniques for those who work with married couples. 253.5.W65

Woods, B. W. *Understanding Suffering.* Grand Rapids: Baker Book House, 1974.
An important book for pastors in that it disabuses the minds of readers of the idea that suffering intensifies misery. 253.5.W85

Neale, Robert. *The Art of Dying.* New York: Harper and Row, 1973.
Covers the subject of death systematically. The inclusion of questionnaires, etc., makes it ideal for use in group discussions. While not an "answer book," its objectivity enables an individual or group to interact with the issues. 128'.5.N25

Chapter 7

SOCIAL AND ECCLESIASTICAL THEOLOGY

Adams, Q. M. *Neither Male nor Female: A Study of the Scriptures.* Ilfracombe, Devon, Eng.: Arthur H. Stockwell, 1973.

In attempting to answer questions such as: What functions does God envisage for women? What responsibilities do they have? And, what limitations (if any) does He impose on them? the author provides one of the best assessments of the Biblical material available today. 261.8'34.AD1

Bruce, Michael, and **G. E. Duffield.** *Why Not? Priesthood and the Ministry of Women.* Appleford, Berkshire, Eng.: Marcham Manor Press, 1972.

Anglican and Episcopalian clergymen discuss the problems associated with the ordination of women to the priesthood. They show an awareness of the history of women's movements in the church from the earliest times to the present, and conclude that women should not be ordained because such action is theologically, exegetically, and historically untenable. 265.4.B83

Casebook on Church and Society. Edited by Keith R. Bridston, *et al.* Nashville: Abingdon Press, 1974.

†Produced by members of the Case-Study Institute of the Episcopal Theological Seminary, these papers direct the reader's attention to ethical, theological, and social problems found in all levels of society. It is valuable for its case-studies, but beyond that it offers little or no help to counselors because the contributors have an unscriptural view of the nature of man. 261.1.C26

Christenson, Laurence. *A Charismatic Approach to Social Action.* Minneapolis: Bethany Fellowship, 1974.

The basic thesis of the author is that involvement in social concerns should be based on the leading of the Holy Spirit rather than the clamors of society. A valuable corrective to prevailing trends in many denominational circles. 261.8'3.C46

Clement, Marcel. *Christ and Revolution.* New Rochelle, NY: Arlington House, 1974.

A well-reasoned rebuttal to the popular idea that Christ was a revolutionary, and that Christianity and radical politics go hand-in-hand. 261.7.C59

Dulles, Avery Robert. *Models of the Church.* Garden City, NY: Doubleday and Company, 1974.

One of the most prolific Roman Catholic writers challenges his readers with the church's mission. He is not as *avant garde* as some outspoken clergymen because his theology remains firmly embedded in the Scripture/Tradition teaching of his church. 262.7.D88

Getz, Gene A. *Sharpening the Focus of the Church.* Chicago: Moody Press, 1974.

Focuses attention on the Biblical qualifications for church leaders; discerns between these qualifications and the use to be made of spiritual gifts; and shows how the work of the church may be enriched and made more effective. 260.G33

Guinnes, Os. *The Dust of Death.* Downers Grove, IL: InterVarsity Press, 1973.

After exposing man's vain search for meaning in the "counter culture" movement, the author proposes a "Third Way," namely, Christianity. He shows how the believer can avoid the extremes of humanism and existentialism by submitting to the authority of Christ. Guinnes describes the dilemmas of Eastern mysticism and the pre-Christian West, and deals with psychedelic drugs and the occult as counterfeits of a true experience with God. 261.83.G94 (Alt. DDC 901.24)

Hamilton, Kenneth, and **Alice Hamilton.** *To Be a Man–To Be a Woman.* Nashville: Abingdon Press, 1975.

An examination of the traditional roles of male and female in contemporary society with an evaluation of the causes which have led up to the present state of affairs. A well-reasoned treatment. 261.8'34.H17

Harkness, Georgia Elma. *Women in Church and Society: A Historical and Theological Inquiry.* Nashville: Abingdon Press, 1974.

Although there are some excellent features in this book, the author's obvious rejection of Biblical revelation leads her first to challenge and then to reinterpret the teachings of the apostle Paul. 261.8'34'2.H22

*Lowell, C. Stanley. *The Great Church-State Fraud.* Washington: Robert B. Luce, 1973.

A sorely needed exposé of the persistent efforts of politicians to alter the First Amendment and bring about an ecclesiastical system which is dependent upon and regulated by the government. 261.7'0973.L95

MacArthur, John, Jr. *The Church, the Body of Christ.* Grand Rapids: Zondervan Publishing House, 1973.

Fails to distinguish between the universal and the local church, but does present important truths relating to the believer's place in the Body. Helpful elucidation is given the gifts of the Spirit and a careful balance is maintained between God's sovereignty and man's responsibility. Recommended. 262.7.M11

McGavran, Donald A. *The Clash Between Christianity and Culture.* Grand Rapids: Baker Book House, 1974.

Attempts to explain how Christians may adjust to another culture while remaining true to Biblical Christianity. Leaves many questions unresolved. 261.1.M17

Monsma, Stephen V. *The Unraveling of America.* Downers Grove, IL: Inter-Varsity Press, 1974.

This critical analysis of government traces the origins of the "unraveling" of the American dream and, after showing the weaknesses of the various political ideologies, proposes an alternative—a progressive realism. Most helpful when read in conjunction with Culver's *Towards a Biblical View of Civil Government.* 261.7.M75

Mayers, Marvin Keene. *Christianity Con-*
fronts Culture: A Strategy for Cross-Culture Evangelism. Grand Rapids: Zondervan Publishing House, 1974.

• Does not deal with evangelism per se, but does provide handy models for cross-cultural communication. 301.1'02'42.M45

Mouw, Richard. *Political Evangelism.* Grand Rapids: Wm. B. Eerdmans Publishing Co., 1973.

This clear, concise, pointed study argues that political action is part of the church's evangelistic task. Working from the perspective of a covenental theologian, Mouw does not make the distinction between the Testaments, and Israel and the church. He overestimates the benefit of community and plays down the possibility that a community may degenerate into tyranny. 261.7.M86

Rahner, Karl. *The Shape of the Church.* Translated by Edward Quinn. London: S.P.C.K., 1974.

† First published in Germany in 1972, this analysis of the situation facing Christendom today is of real value because it presents the latest attempts of Romanism to make an impact on the masses. It describes the way teaching should be conducted and the best means for the church to regain its lost authority. 260.R12

Scanzoni, Letha, and **Nancy Hardesty.** *All We're Meant to Be.* Waco, TX: Word Books, 1975.

An attempt to form a Biblical approach to Women's Lib within the evangelical framework. It affirms the equality of women in leadership roles in the church and home. The handling of Scripture is at places strained in this analysis of multifaceted womanhood. 261.8'34'12.SC6

Schillebeeck, Edward. *The Mission of the Church.* New York: Seabury Press, 1973.

In this provocative work, the author, a Dutch theologian, shows his disenchantment with many of the practices of Roman Catholic Church. 262.SCH3

Tavard, George Henri. *Woman in Christian Tradition.* South Bend, IN: University of Notre Dame Press, 1973.

Part of the growing corpus of literature on the place of women in church and society. Concentrates on the teachings of the Church Fathers and sees in the unmarried state a solution to the problems of the age. Roman Catholic. 261.8'34.T19

Public Worship, Ceremonies, Ordinances

Cochrane, Arthur. *Eating and Drinking with Jesus.* Philadelphia: Westminster Press, 1974.

† An ethical and quasi-Biblical study of the Lord's Supper. 234.163.C64

Eller, Vernard. *In Place of Sacraments: A Study of Baptism and the Lord's Supper.* Grand Rapids: Wm. B. Eerdmans Publishing Co., 1972.

A vigorous critique of what the author considers the unbiblical method of observing the church ordinances, coupled with suggestions for old and new ways to enhance them. 265.EL5

Robertson, James Douglas. *The Minister's Worship Handbook.* Grand Rapids: Baker Book House, 1974.

An innovative manual replete with programs and prayers. 264'.002.R54

Chapter 8

MISSIONS AND EVANGELISM

Beyerhaus, Peter. *Shaken Foundations.* Grand Rapids: Zondervan Publishing House, 1973.

Designed for students of missions, this book may be read with profit by all evangelicals. It documents the rise of theological liberalism in Germany and describes its tragic consequences, first in its approach to the Bible, and second in its outworking in missions and evangelism. 266.'001.B46

Coggins, Wade T. *So That's What Missions Is All About.* Chicago: Moody Press, 1975.

A veteran missionary discusses the *sine quo non* of missions and mission support. For laymen. Recommended. 266'.001.C65

Collins, Marjorie A. *A Manual for Accepted Missionary Candidates.* Pasadena, CA: William Carey Library, 1972.

An important volume for all who plan to go to the mission field. 266'.001.C69

————. *A Manual for Missionaries on Furlough.* Pasadena, CA: William Carey Library, 1972.

A practical guide for missionaries, particularly those facing their first furlough. 266'.008.C69

Griffiths, Michael C. *Who Really Sends the Missionary?* Chicago: Moody Press, 1974.

Pastors of missionary-minded churches will welcome this handy book. It delineates the church's task and encourages each local assembly to face up to its responsibility. 266'.001.G87

Hefley, James C., and **Marti Hefley.** *Uncle Cam.* Waco, TX: Word Books, 1974.

A sympathetic presentation of William Cameron Townsend, founder of the Wycliffe Bible Translator/Summer Institute of Linguistic and Jungle and Aviation Radio Service

(JAARS). Includes his reasons for working with Pentecostals and the many internal and external controversies which have plagued the mission. 266'.023.0924.T66H

Hendricks, Howard George with **Ted Miller.** *Say It with Love.* Wheaton: Victor Books, 1973.

An important, *new* approach to personal evangelism. Ideal for discussion groups. 248.5.H38

Hodges, Melvin L. *A Guide to Church Planting.* Chicago: Moody Press, 1974.

A contemporary discussion of principles which have engaged the attention of missiologists for many years. 266'.08.H66

International Congress on World Evangelization. *Let the Earth Hear His Voice.* Edited by J. D. Douglas. Minneapolis: World Wide Publications, 1975.

This "official reference volume" contains the papers (and responses) delivered at the congress in Lausanne, Switzerland, in 1974. Some of the contributors are well known, and others make their debut in this volume. The work as a whole is of uneven value, but its message is sorely needed. 269.2.IN8D

*Kane, J. Herbert.** *Understanding Christian Missions.* Grand Rapids: Baker Book House, 1974.

Describes the contemporary problems facing Christian missions and explains the present-day oppotunities. Well deserves the status of a college or seminary text, and should be "required reading" for all missionary candidates. 266.K13U

————. *Winds of Change in the Christian Mission.* Chicago: Moody Press, 1973.

These exciting chapters by a veteran missionary provide honest answers to young people's questions and present the challenge of today's missionary opportunities in a clear, positive light. 266K13W

McQuilken, J. Robertson. *Measuring the Church Growth Movement.* Revised ed. Chicago: Moody Press, 1974.

A cautious examination of the five presuppositions underlying the Church Growth Movement. Concludes that the movement is Biblical but fails to provide a solid theological critique of its basic position. 266'.001.M24

Nevius, John Livingstone. *Planting and Development of Missionary Churches.* Nutley, NJ: Presbyterian and Reformed Publishing Co., 1974.

Although first published in 1885, this book contains an abundance of practical counsel that is still relevant today. 266'.01.N41

*Olsen, Viggo with **Jeanette Lockerbie.**

Daktar: Diplomat of Bangladesh. Chicago: Moody Press, 1973.

An exacting study of the life of a dedicated medical missionary among the poor of Pakistan before it became the world's 147th nation. 954.9'205.0L8

*Peters, George W. *A Biblical Theology of Missions.* Chicago: Moody Press, 1973.

Directs attention to the fundamental issues of missions today and draws from the Scriptures God's "blueprint" for missionary principles and strategy. 266.01.P44

Tippett, Alan Richard, ed. *God, Man and Church Growth.* Grand Rapids: Wm. B. Eerdmans Publishing Co., 1974.

A *Festschrift* in honor of the famous missiologist, Donald Anderson McGavran. Contains twenty-nine essays on a wide range of topics which pinpoint many of the crucial areas of concern today. 266'001.M17.T49

Chapter 9

CHRISTIAN EDUCATION

Corbett, Janice M., ed. *Explore; Resources for Junior Highs in the Church.* Valley Forge: Judson Press, 1974.

Geared to the needs of this age group and aimed at developing their spiritual sensitivity. Will be of real help to all who work in the junior high department. 268.433.C81

Cully, Iris V. *Change, Conflict and Self-Determination: Next Steps in Religious Education.* Philadelphia: Westminster Press, 1972.

An analysis of how teaching methods within our churches may be altered to keep pace with the forces for change within our society. 268.372.C91

Gangel, Kenneth O. *24 Ways to Improve Your Teaching.* Wheaton; Victor Books, 1974.

Ideal for use by DCEs in training groups, or to give to aspiring teachers. 371.102.G15

Lefever, Marlene D. *Turnabout Teaching.* Elgin, IL: David C. Cook, 1974.

Part of the publisher's "Christian Education series," this handy manual contains innovative ideas for today's teachers. 268.433.L52

McDaniel, Elsiebeth with **Lawrence O. Richards.** *You and Preschoolers.* Chicago: Moody Press, 1975.

Another important volume which DCEs and those who work with preschoolers will find invaluable. 268.432.M14

Robinson, James Herman. *Bulletin Board Ideas.* St. Louis: Concordia Publishing House, 1973.

A practical handbook designed to spur creativity. 268.6.R56

*Ryrie, Charles Caldwell. *Easy-to-Give Object Lessons.* Chicago: Moody Press, 1974.

These simple object lessons will be welcomed by all who work with children. 268.635.R99E 1974

*Zuck, Roy B., and **R. E. Clark, eds.** *Childhood Education in the Church.* Chicago: Moody Press, 1975.

This volume (with *Youth and the Church* and *Adult Education in the Church*) completes a trilogy surveying Christian education from the different age levels. Designed to educate, challenge, and direct the activities of those responsible for children in the church. Recommended. 268.432.Z8

Chapter 10

CHURCH HISTORY

General Reference Works

The Encyclopedia of World Methodism. Edited by Nolan B. Harmon. 2 vols. Nashville: Abingdon Press, 1974.

Replete with information on all boards and agencies, and containing extensive appendices. Also provides data on the prominent people and places, doctrines and practices of Methodism. 287.EN1H

*The New International Dictionary of the Christian Church. Edited by J. D. Douglas. Grand Rapids: Zondervan Publishing House, 1974.

While representative of the latest international scholarship, and being far more evangelical than Cross's *Oxford Dictionary of the Christian Church,* this volume nevertheless lacks the decisive quality of a consistently conservative work. The articles make available to busy pastors a wealth of practical and illustrative material. 270.03.N42 1974 (Alt. DDC 203)

*The Oxford Dictionary of the Christian Church. Edited by F. L. Cross and E. A. Livingstone. 2d ed. London: Oxford University Press, 1974.

†This predominantly Anglican dictionary of the Christian church was first published in 1958. The articles are arranged alphabetically and include biographical, theological, and ecclesiastical themes. Many have valuable bibliographies appended to them. The new edition includes data from Vatican II, a chronological listing of popes, recent trends within different denominations, and more. 270.03.0X2.C88 1974

The Church in America

Benne, Robert, and **Philip Hefner.** *Defining America.* Philadelphia: Fortress Press, 1974.

Building upon the three basic American values of freedom, initiative, and opportunity, the writers reappraise Christianity in the United States and attempt to chart a course for the future. In spite of their pessimistic outlook and lack of eschatological awareness, theirs is still a work worth consulting. 917.3.B43

Brill, Earl H. *The Future of the American Past.* New York: Seabury Press, 1974.

An attempt on the part of an Episcopalian to find out what has gone wrong with the American dream and provide guidelines whereby Christians may become better citizens. Sociological. 209.73.B76

Cairns, Earle E. *V. Raymond Edman: In the Presence of the King.* Chicago: Moody Press, 1972.

The authorized biography of one of America's great Christian statesmen. 268.573.ED5.C12

Clebsch, William A. *American Religious Thought: A History.* Chicago: University of Chicago Press, 1973.

This history of the philosophy of religion in

America concentrates on three principal figures—J. Edwards, R. W. Emerson, and W. James—and claims that these men abandoned a "moralistic spirituality" for an "aesthetic spirituality." Helpful for its analysis, but deficient in its theology. 200.9'73.C58

*Edwards, Jonathan. *The Great Awakening.* Vol. 4. *The Works of Jonathan Edwards.* Edited by C. C. Goen. New Haven: Yale University Press, 1972.

This book focuses attention on a movement begun in New England between 1735-51. In presenting Edwards's material the editor has endeavored to delineate a series of historical developments in and through which the great preacher's thought was formulated. This volume, therefore, becomes a narrative construction of the history of the times and enables the reader to sense the process of reflection which Edwards followed. 285.873.ED9G 1972

Endy, Melvin B. *William Penn and Early Quakerism.* Princeton: Princeton University Press, 1973.

A detailed examination of Penn's relationship with the Quakers and the development of his own religious convictions. Contains some surprising statements about the origin and development of the movement. 289.6.P37.EN2

Holbrook, Clyde A. *The Ethics of Jonathan Edwards: Morality and Aesthetics.* Ann Arbor: University of Michigan Press, 1973.

The author blends Edwards's theological objectivism and practical subjectivism into a work which reveals not only the New England minister's Puritan theology, but his Lockean psychology as well. The truths thus gleaned are then applied to the areas of morality and aesthetics. 285.8'0924.ED9.H69

Gaustad, Edwin Scott. *Dissent in American Religion.* Chicago: University of Chicago Press, 1973.

This analysis of "dissent" in a highly pluralistic society claims that religion today is passé and that a "conservative reaction" to prevalent trends is the only way to recover a lost dynamism. 200.9'73.G23

Henry, Stuart C. *Unvanquished Puritan.* Grand Rapids: Wm. B. Eerdmans Publishing Co., 1973.

A discerning discussion of Lyman Beecher and his famous family (including the authoress of *Uncle Tom's Cabin,* and Isabella Beecher, an early crusader for female liberation). 285.9'0924.B39.H39

*Hudson, Winthrop Still. *Religion in America.* 2d ed. New York: Charles

Scribner's Sons, 1973.

†Updates the author's 1965 survey of American religious history, by including a study of the occult, the charismatic movement, and the impact of Vatican II on contemporary Roman Catholicism. 200'.973.H86

*Jones, James William. *The Shattered Synthesis: New England Puritanism Before the Great Awakening.* New Haven: Yale University Press, 1973.

An important assessment of the issues the Puritans faced and the manner in which they dealt with them. 974.4'02.J71

Kelley, Dean M. *Why Conservative Churches Are Growing.* New York: Harper and Row, 1972.

A sociological study of the attitudes (rather than the doctrines and practices) of "conservative" churches, including Mormons and other sects. Needs to be read in the light of Murch's *The Protestant Revolt.* 280.07.K28

Sweet, William Warren. *The Story of Religion in America.* Grand Rapids: Baker Book House, 1973.

First published in 1930, this old, reliable standby takes readers on an excursus through the many and varied aspects of American religious life. 261.7'0973.S3

Simonson, Harold P. *Jonathan Edwards: Theologian of the Heart.* Grand Rapids: Wm. B. Eerdmans Publishing Co., 1974.

A brilliant literary and theological analysis of one of America's leading figures. Draws principles from Edwards's messages and applies them to the needs of the present hour. 285.8'73.ED9.S5

Towns, Elmer L. *Is the Day of the Denomination Dead?* Nashville: T. Nelson and Sons, 1973.

Towns contends that although denominationalism may have made a contribution in the past, urbanization, advancing technology, and a rapidly changing society, now make it more of a hindrance to the advance of the gospel than a help. This book should be read along with Murch's *The Protestant Revolt* and Brown's *Protest of a Troubled Protestant.* 280.07'73.T66

Williams, John Bickerton. *The Lives of Philip and Matthew Henry.* Carlisle, PA: Banner of Truth Trust, 1974.

Containing two volumes in one, these accounts of a notable father and his illustrious son provide an important study of the effect of godliness in the home and the way in which a parent's spiritual commitment and practical wisdom influenced his children and are forever enshrined in his one son's famous *Commentary*. 285.2'42.H39.W67

Wiersbe, Warren W. *William Culbertson: A Man of God*. Chicago: Moody Press, 1974.

This biography captures the deeply devotional spirit of William Culbertson, carefully describes the path God chose in preparing him for the work he performed, and readily reveals the way in which he was used to influence young and old alike. 285.3.C91W

The Church in Europe

Crossley, Robert. *Luther and the Peasant's War*. Jericho, NY: Exposition Press, 1974.
A careful presentation of Luther's actions and reactions. 943'.031.C88

Donaldson, George. *The Scottish Reformation*. Cambridge: At the University Press, 1972.
A brilliantly written treatment of the way in which Protestantism was established in Scotland. 285.241.D71

* *The Works of John Fletcher*. Hobe Sound, FL: Hobe Sound Bible College Press, 1974.
Long out of print, this material by one of the foremost apologists of early Methodism will be welcomed by evangelicals of all denominations. 287.141.F63

Halevy, Elie. *The Birth of Methodism in England*. Translated and edited by Bernard Semmuel. Chicago: University of Chicago Press, 1971.
Based on two French journal articles, these studies make an important contribution to the study of early Methodism. 287'.142.H13

Hillerbrand, Hans Joachim. *The World of the Reformation*. New York: Charles Scribner's Sons, 1973.
In surveying the Reformation era, the author successfully combines narrative history with interpretive insights. His information on the interplay between religion and society makes this a most rewarding study. 270.6.H55

Hunter, Archibald Macbride. *P. T. Forsyth*. Philadelphia: Westminster Press, 1974.
A brief but important monograph on the theological contribution of one of the great

leaders in the Congregational church in England. 285.8'0924.F77.H91

McNeill, John Thomas. *The Celtic Churches: A History, A. D. 200 to 1200*. Chicago: University of Chicago Press, 1974.
An important study of a long-neglected missionary-minded movement. 274.M23

Sider, Ronald. *Andreas Bodenstein von Karlstadt*. Leiden, The Netherlands: E. J. Brill, 1974.
This opponent of Luther's receives a sympathetic and balanced treatment with the result that he adds to (rather than detracts from) the luster which has come to be associated with the great Reformer. 284.1'0924.K14.S1

Southern, Richard William. *Western Society and the Church in the Middle Ages*. Grand Rapids: Wm. B. Eerdmans Publishing Co., 1972.
This important survey of eight hundred years of history concentrates attention on the connection between the religious organizations and the social environment of the medieval church. 270.4.S8

**C. H. Spurgeon Autobiography*. Vol. 2 *The Full Harvest, 1860-1892*. Edinburgh: The Banner of Truth Trust, 1973.

This long-awaited companion volume to *The Early Years* (1962), will stimulate, encourage, and edify those presently engaged in a pastoral ministry and challenge those who are preparing for it. 286.142.S9 V.2

Toon, Peter. *God's Statesman: The Life and Work of John Owen*. Grand Rapids: Zondervan Publishing House, 1973.

An important biography of one of the leading theologians of the Puritan era. 285.342.0W2.T61

Wilkie, William E. *The Cardinal Protectors of England: Rome and the Tudors Before the*

Reformation. New York: Cambridge University Press, 1974.
A painstaking discussion of the period from 1485 to 1539, focusing special attention on the protectors in office until Henry's divorce and remarriage in 1533. 282.42.W65

Sects and Cults

*****Davis, John J.** *Contemporary Counterfeits.* Grand Rapids: Baker Book House, 1973.
An analysis of the various manifestations of occultism in the lesser-known cults. 133.D29

Ebon, Martin. *The Devil's Bride —Exorcism: Past and Present.* New York: Harper and Row, 1974.
Containing case histories of exorcism as well as an abundance of material documenting man's obsession with Satanism and the occult. Majors on the sensational and lacks Biblical data. 133.3.EB7

*****Martin, Walter Ralston.** *The Kingdom of the Occult.* Santa Ana, CA: Vision House, 1974.
A comprehensive examination of the history and theology of occultism. 133.M36

Montgomery, John Warwick. *Principalities and Powers: The World of the Occult.* Minneapolis: Bethany Fellowship, 1974.
A candid historic and contemporary appraisal of the many and varied forms of Satanism. 133.M76

*****Unger, Merrill Frederick.** *Beyond the Crystal Ball.* Chicago: Moody Press, 1973.
Provides a balanced treatment of the limitations of occultism, links Biblical prediction with world events, and exposes the origin, power, and delusion of Satansim. 133.3.UN3

Warnke, Mike with **Dave Balsiger** and **Les Jones.** *The Satan-seller.* Plainfield, NJ: Logos International, 1972.
An interesting and highly dramatic personal odyssey which exposes the dangers of Satan worship. Deserves to be read by every parent and teenager. 248'.2.W24

Chantry, Walter J. *Signs of the Apostles: An Examination of the New Pentecostalism.* London: Banner of Truth Trust, 1973.
This concise critique of the charismatic movement claims that adherence to and involvement in neo-Pentecostalism necessitates an implicit denial of the doctrine of the authority of the Scriptures and the all-sufficiency of the Word of God. 289.9.C36

Hollenweger, Walter J. *The Pentecostals: The Charismatic Movement in the Churches.* Translated by R. A. Wilson. Minneapolis: Augsburg Publishing House, 1972.
A comprehensive and scholarly book which begins with historical sketches of the movement in the United States and elsewhere, and then analyzes the beliefs of adherents. The author, a member of the Pentecostal church, is obviously sympathetic to their cause. Highly informative. 289.9.H72

Jorstad, Erling, ed. *The Holy Spirit in Today's Church.* Nashville: Abingdon Press, 1973.
A handbook of neo-Pentecostalism which attempts to answer the basic questions raised about the movement. 248.173.J76

Kildahl, John P. *The Psychology of Speaking in Tongues.* New York: Harper and Row, 1972.
Based on reports of glossolalia, personal interviews, tapes, and other research, this approach to new-Pentecostalism seeks to provide a factual answer to questions such as: Who is involved? Why do they speak in tongues? What does it all mean? 234.1.K55

Samarin, William J. *Tongues of Men and Angels.* New York: Macmillan Co., 1972.
A thorough assessment of the modern *glossolalia* movement. Among the conclusions reached by the author are that the phenomenon in Acts 2 was an example of *xenoglossolalia,* and that the modern counterpart of this has a beneficial effect because it makes the individual feel good. Valuable for its linguistic analysis of *glossolalia,* but deficient in exegetical and theological expertise. 289.9.S4

Hopkins, Joseph Martin. *The Armstrong Empire.* Grand Rapids: Wm. B. Eerdmans Publishing Co., 1974.
A capable handling of the history of Herbert W. Armstrong and his Worldwide Church of God, but does not include a clear deliniation of Armstrong's doctrine. 289.9.H77

Kaufman, Robert. *Inside Scientology: How*

I Joined Scientology and Became Superhuman. New York: Olympia Press, 1972.

A candid exposé which deserves to be read by all who have been approached by adherents to this movement. 131.35.K16

Larson, Bob. *The Guru.* Denver: The Author, 1974.

A candid polemic against the claims and teachings of the teenage Maharaj Ji. 133.42.L32

Chapter 11

COMPARATIVE RELIGIONS

Judaism

*Josephus, Flavius. *The Works of Flavius Josephus*. Translated by William Whiston. 4 vols. Grand Rapids: Baker Book House, 1974.

A classic. Valuable as a guide in the study of the OT and helpful in understanding the history of the Jewish people. 933.J77 1974

Levine, Baruch A. *In the Presence of the Lord*. Leiden, The Netherlands: E. J. Brill, 1974.

An exacting study of sacrificial systems in Ugaritic and Israelite religions. 296.L57

Neusner, Jacob. *The Idea of Purity in Ancient Judaism*. Leiden, The Netherlands: E. J. Brill, 1974.

This brilliant treatise by a noted Jewish historian draws attention to the Biblical basis for purity in the OT and its post-Biblical practice in Judaism. A careful perusal of Neusner's work will add a new dimension to the study of the OT. 291.22.N39

————, ed. *Understanding Rabbinic Judaism from Talmudic to Modern Times*. New York: Ktav Publishing House, 1974.

Containing chapters contributed by modern Jewish historians and theologians, this work illustrates the way in which Rabbinic Judaism laid the foundations of Jewish history. Casts an abundance of light on many OT concepts and practices. 296.N39

Nickelsburg, George W. E. *Resurrection, Immortality, and Eternal Life in Intertestamental Judiasm*. Harvard Theological Studies. Cambridge: Harvard University Press, 1972.

An important contribution. 296.3'3.N53

Novak, David. *Law and Theology in Judaism*. New York: Ktav Publishing House, 1974.

The first and last chapters of this work are of great importance to non-Jewish readers. The first emphasizes the fact that it is possible to understand Judaism only as one understands the relationship between the *halakhah* ("law") and *aggadah* ("theology"). The last discusses the relationship of faith and knowledge. The chapters in between elaborate on chapter 1 and are more distinctively Jewish in orientation. A revealing and rewarding work. 296.1'79.N85

Pearlman, Moshe. *The Maccabees*. New York: Macmillan Co., 1974.

A well-illustrated portrayal of Hebrew history during the inter-testamental period. 933.M12.P31

Sabourin, Leopold. *Priesthood: A Comparative Study*. Leiden, The Netherlands: E. J. Brill, 1973.

In this important study a Jesuit priest investigates the nature and function of the priesthood in ancient religions. Focuses attention primarily on the Aaronic order. A final chapter is devoted to "Jesus the High Priest." As a comparative study, this work has a great deal to commend it. Pertinent and revealing. 291.61.S1

Schürer, Emil. *The History of the Jewish People in the Age of Jesus Christ*. Revised and edited by Gaza Vermas and Fergus Miller. Edinburgh: T. and T. Clark, 1973–.

Still in progress, this revision is designed to update this magisterial work which has long been out of print. 933.SCH8 1973

Vermes, Geza. *Scripture and Tradition in Judaism.* Studia Post-Biblica. 2d revised ed. Leiden, The Netherlands: E. J. Brill, 1973.

A detailed study of *haggadic* exegesis highlighting eight incidents in the Bible. 221.8.V59

World Religions

Historical Atlas of the Religions of the World. Edited by Ishra'il Ragi al Faruqi. New York: Macmillan Publishing Co., 1974.

†Interspersed throughout this handsome volume are essays on the history of each religion—their growth, and other interesting phenomena relating to their practices. Beautiful black-and-white pictures, and helpful chronological charts, bibliographies, appendixes, and indexes further enhance the usefulness of this important work. 912.12.H62

Parrinder, Geoffrey. *A Dictionary of Non-Christian Religions.* Philadelphia: Westminster Press, 1973.

Helps the researcher find reliable data on a wide range of religious themes. 290.3.P24

Catoir, John T. *The Way People Pray.* New York: Paulist Press. 1974.

A brief introduction to the history of religious belief. 291.C29

Eliade, Mircea. *Death, Afterlife and Eschatology.* New York: Harper and Row, 1974.

A secular approach to the historical development of these doctrines in pagan religions. Insightful. 291.09.EL5

———. *Gods, Goddesses, and Myths of Creation.* New York: Harper and Row, 1974.

Containing part of the author's *From Primitives to Zen,* this study focuses on the cosmological beliefs of pagan societies. 291.2.EL5

Beyer, Stephan. *The Cult of Tara.* Berkeley: University of California Press, 1974.

This scholarly appraisal of Buddhist origins and ritual concentrates on the goddess, Tara, and her influence on Tibetan life and thought. 294.3'4'38.B46

Huxley, Francis. *The Way of the Sacred.* Garden City, NY: Doubleday and Co., 1974.

An assessment of the place of symbols, rites, and ceremonies in religious worship. Sacramental. 291.H98

Ingrams, Doreen. *Mosques and Minarets.* St. Paul: EMC Corporation, 1974.

A revealing discussion of the basic teachings of Islam, illustrating through photographs and narration the unifying effect of their beliefs on the Arab nations of the Middle East. 297.IN4

Jung, Leo. *Fallen Angels in Jewish, Christian, and Mohammedan Literature.* New York: Ktav Publishing House, 1974.

Reprinted from the 1926 edition, this treatise provides an informative, comparative study of demonology. 291.2'16.J95 1974

MacDonell, Arthur Anthony. *Vedic Mythology.* New York: Gordon Press, 1974.

Based on an earlier German work by George Buhler, this analysis of Hindu beliefs will prove to be of real value to those whose ministry brings them into contact with these primitive beliefs. 294.1.M14

Miller, William McElwee. *The Baha'i Faith: Its History and Teaching.* South Pasadena, CA: William Carey Library, 1974.

An excellent exposé of this fast-growing sect. Of special value to collegiates who have been invited to join this syncretistic but anti-Christian group. 297.89.M61

Shaku, Soyen. *Zen for Americans.* Translated by Daisetz Teitars Suzuki. La Salle, IL: Open Court, 1974.

This reprint of a 1906 publication is designed to take advantage of the resurgence of interest in Oriental mysticism and make Buddhism more appealing to Occidentals. 294.3'08.SH1

Watt, William Montgomery. *Muhammad: Prophet and Statesman.* New York: Oxford University Press, 1974.

A full treatment even though it gives evidence of being an abridgement of the author's earlier work. 297.63.W34

AUTHOR INDEX

TITLE INDEX